MW00812296

FEEDBACK MENTALITY

The key to unlocking and unleashing
your full potential

DR. SHANITA WILLIAMS

Dedication

Lord, in your Word you say, "For I know the plans I have for you…" Thank you for making plans for me and believing me to be capable and worthy enough to carry out the plans you have for my life. Thank you for the tests and the testimony that gave birth to this work. Thank you for the opportunity to be the vessel that carries this message forward. It is my hope that hearts and minds will be positively impacted and that people will be able to live out the plans and purpose that you have for them as well. All of this is to the Glory of God.

This book is dedicated to my three beautiful children: Josan, Jolie, and Jonay.

Remember, your thoughts are powerful!

If you can conceive it in your mind, you can hold it in your hands.

Dream big and get your hands ready!

If you find that your dream is too big for your hands alone,

Call it a blessing and ask your siblings to lend you their hands.

Individually, your dreams will change you.

Collectively, your dreams will change the world!

Go change the world, Josan, Jolie, and Jonay!

I love you so much and I believe in each of you!

Table of Contents

Introduction

Feedback is ubiquitous—it is literally all around us. It has quietly cemented itself into the daily nuances of every human interaction that it is now like air; we take it in subconsciously and have no idea how it moves throughout our bodies and influences our thoughts and behaviors. Feedback has played an integral role in shaping our performance, the communities in which we live, the policies we create, and our relationships with others. If used correctly, it is an effective tool that can be a catalyst for growth. If we want to influence behavior change, organizational change, systems change, or societal change, we must improve our ability to deliver, receive, process, and apply feedback.

While feedback is a part of our everyday lives, many lack the necessary skills to leverage feedback around them to facilitate their growth and the growth of others. This is not a judgement; it's really based in fact. Think about it. When were you taught how to effectively utilize feedback? Do you remember having a course in elementary school, junior high, high school, or college? What about when you got your first job? Where you trained at church or when you joined the local sports team? Chance are, you've given a lot of feedback to others and received a whole lot of feedback from others with little to no education or training on how to do so effectively. It's not your fault; our society has not prioritized it as a core skill or competency that should be sought after. Because of this, it makes engaging in a feedback conversation uncomfortable and even risky as people recklessly fumble their way through sending and receiving feedback that can impact one's self-esteem, relationships, performance, and quite literally, one's life.

For the last fifteen years, I have coached, mentored, and trained hundreds of individuals with an underlying focus on understanding the human experience and creating conditions that empower people to grow and reach their fullest potential. I have learned that no matter your age, race, gender identity, industry, management level, tenure, or relationship, feedback is central to the human experience; we might not all want it but we most certainly need it. Poorly delivered feedback can hurt—and hurt people hurt people. This vicious cycle of poorly delivered feedback creates mental and emotional obstacles that have the potential to prevent people from living out their purpose.

Without the skills to effectively leverage feedback, organizations will struggle to meet the needs of their customers and employees. Without the skills to effectively leverage feedback, athletes might give up on pursuing their passion. Without the skills to effectively leverage feedback, leaders stop leading and start managing. Without the skills to effectively leverage feedback, students may believe they are incapable of success. Without the skills to leverage feedback, long-term relationships come to an end prematurely. Without the skills to effectively leverage feedback, you might stop believing in your ability to reach your dreams.

I can teach you to effectively handle feedback—and all of the answers are literally in your hands. In this book, you'll learn how to effectively deliver feedback to others, receive feedback from others, process the internal narrative attached to feedback, and apply the feedback to your everyday life. We will examine your attitude and mindset around feedback, build your mental and emotional strength to handle feedback, and provide you with strategies to prevent you from becoming mentally and emotionally exhausted from feedback fatigue. Thank you for joining the journey. You're in for an exciting ride.

CHAPTER ONE

What is Feedback?

"Don't tell me the sky's the limit when there are footprints on the moon."—Paul Brandt

Given the right conditions, a seed and caterpillar can grow and become something new. In their newly evolved state, they experience the world differently, creating new meaning and purpose for their lives. Can you imagine speaking to a caterpillar about its potential to become a butterfly? Imagine the response you'd get when you told it about all the places it could fly in a single day, or that their ability to collect and carry pollen to fruit, vegetables, and flowers was critical to maintaining the ecosystem? I imagine that it might be difficult for the caterpillar to understand the vast possibilities of their potential even if they saw other caterpillars transform right before them.

Can you imagine having a conversation with the seed before its planted? Can you imagine the response you'd receive when you told the seed it had the potential to become a 100 foot Redwood Tree, that it would provide the oxygen needed to sustain human life, and that it could bear fruit that would go on to feed hundreds if not thousands of families? Do you think the tiny seed knows the potential it has within?

When it comes to human potential, you can grow and become something new. While a seed requires soil, sunlight, and water, human beings need feedback. Feedback is the gateway to helping you become an improved version of yourself and evolve in many facets of the human experience. Human beings have a potential that is vast, infinite, limitless, and unbounded by any social construct or expectation other than your own. Your potential is predicated on your ability to receive, process, and apply the feedback given to you effectively. Hold on to the wrong feedback, and you limit your potential. Leverage the right feedback, and you're on your way to discovering the best parts of yourself, opening up endless future possibilities.

What if I told you that you had the potential to become the most beloved musician in the world? Or that you'd eventually find the cure for cancer, saving thousands of lives? Or that your commitment to social justice would create laws the ensure equity and justice for countless marginalized groups of people. Do you believe you have the potential to accomplish those things? In many instances, the human potential goes undiscovered and unrealized simply because we are unaware that we have it and are unsure how to tap into it.

Feedback is the gateway to discovering your potential. The feedback stored in your mind becomes the epicenter that drives your thoughts, feelings, behaviors, and subsequent results in your life. If you were to stop and examine your thinking, you'd have insight about where you are on the path towards reaching your full potential. Also, you can more than likely trace your thoughts about your potential back to feedback that was given to you by others or yourself. Is your inability to effectively handle feedback limiting your potential? Is your ability to deliver feedback limiting someone's potential? Once you develop a feedback mentality, you have the keys you need to unlock and unleash your full potential as well as the potential of others.

What comes to mind when you hear the word "feedback"? For some, it sparks feelings of curiosity, growth, and gratitude. But for many, the term "feedback" conjures up feelings of anxiety, fear, and overall inadequacy. In the simplest of terms, many are afraid of feedback. Some are so afraid that they avoid it, loath giving it, have a hard time leveraging it, and some are even holding their breath while receiving it. How can one word hold so much power? How can one word tell your brain you need it but in the same breath, make you afraid of it? How can one word create such a varied emotional response that people even avoid using the word altogether to avoid triggering the flight-or-fight response?

In order to understand the power of feedback, we must first start with a fundamental understanding of what it is.

Feedback is information that gives insight into how one perceives something or someone. Feedback is "the transmission of evaluative or corrective information about an action, event, or process to the original or controlling source" (Merriam-Webster, 2020). It is information that has the potential to influence future performance. The most powerful word in all three definitions is "information." Feedback is information. Information is defined as "facts provided or learned about something or someone" (Merriam-Webster, 2020). Newton's Third Law of Motion asserts that every action has a reaction. I believe every behavior carries with it information that will trigger a reaction from someone—either positive or negative. It is feedback that helps bring clarity and understanding about what we should or should not do, becoming a vital part of our decision-making process.

The challenge with feedback is that many have a hard time identifying the feedback they receive if it is not packaged with the statement, "this is feedback." That means, all of the other feedback does not really "count" in their minds. In my experience of leading and developing others, I can point to many occasions where employees said, "I wish I had more feedback," only to draw their attention to the numerous examples where I provided guidance, redirection, correction, alternative perspectives, questions to ponder, affirmation, admiration, and even encouragement. Many find themselves walking down feedback memory lane pulling up documentation just to prove that they did indeed give feed-back—reviewing archived emails, text messages, or replaying back an entire conversation like it was transcribed. When the feed-back recipient finally makes the connection that they did indeed receive feedback, they usually gave a look or response that was equivalent to "oh, yeah I remember that now," leaving the person on the other side of the table relieved! The conversation usually ends with the recipient alluding to something along the lines of "you should have been more explicit that this was feedback." This reaction became a huge learning moment for me: *there was gap between the desire for feedback and the employee's ability to identify feedback.*

If you think feedback must include a "this is feedback" clause and a formal setting to indicate that feedback is coming, you might be waiting until your formal annual performance review and by then, it is too late. Now, let's be honest, there are some leaders that avoid giving feedback until the review process because they simply lack the confidence, skill, or the desire to do so. We will talk about that later. However, feedback is information and it is all around us. Your coach, your doctor, your teacher, your sister, your manager, your child, and many others are sending feedback all the time, but you have to have the ability to hear it without the accompanying statement, "This is feedback" in order to harness it.

One day, I was asked to prepare a presentation that would be reviewed by my peers so that we could ensure we were aligned with the goals of an upcoming training. As I walked everyone through the presentation, I noticed that one of the leaders was having a hard time with what I was sharing. How did I know this? The look on his face sent some strong information signals that it was time to pause and lean in to understand and address his concerns. I paused and asked for his thoughts and he gave me insights that changed the entire flow of the training…in a positive way. That training session ended up being one of the highest rated trainings I delivered to date. To this day, I think about that moment and wonder what would have happened if I did not pick up on information that was in front of me and give him space to provide me with a new perspective. Sure, the training would have been delivered and I am sure it would have gone well, but it definitely would not have been as successful. I am very grateful for his perspective and feedback, even if I had to listen hard to catch it.

I had another feedback experience that was also unique. I was sitting on my bed with a bowl of popcorn in my lap and the remote control in my hand. I was binge-watching Game of Thrones and I wasn't going to miss a scene! You know that feeling when you're in the zone and you can block out anything and anyone when you're hyper-focused on something? That was me—Game of Thrones-focused. I think I watched like five seasons in like two days…if you can imagine. During my marathon watching spree, I heard the voice of one of my children, "Mommy, you said you were going to play with me." I apparently kept promising my little one that I would play with her after this "episode" was over. I don't even remember how many episodes she had to wait.

Poor thing grabbed me by the face so that I could lock eyes with her. And just like that, the spell was broken and I realized what was happening. Yup, that was feedback. My daughter wanted some quality time and she deserved it. She was giving me feedback and holding me accountable to my word. Game of Thrones had to wait.

I was able to identify feedback, take the cues, and adjust my behavior. I knew that many people struggled with simply identifying feedback, so it inspired me to take a deeper dive into the feedback experience and think more intently about the ideologies that surrounded the notion of feedback altogether. If we are able to get the most out of feedback, we have to be willing to explore some of the myths and false expectations that are surrounding this powerful tool. By dispelling the myths, we might be in a better position to truly see the feedback in front of us.

Feedback Myths

To further expand your understanding of feedback, we will explore the Ten Myths that many have had about feedback. These myths prevent us from getting the maximum value from feedback opportunities and could inevitably stunt our ability to make behavioral, organizational, and societal change. Which myths have you heard?

Ten Feedback Myths

Myth #1: Feedback is limited to a specific time of year

When we look at the ecosystem in which feedback occurs, it's only natural for people to believe that feedback is limited to specific points in time. For example, many organizations have annual performance appraisals as a part of their performance review process, and some hold all of the feedback or only look for feedback during this time. Most educational institutions have end-of-course evaluations for their faculty or midterms and progress reports for their students, further reinforcing that these are the times that you have to either provide or look for feedback. When it comes to family and feedback, some wait to provide feedback until the annual holiday celebration because it's the only time that they will see you face-to-face.

While these moments are great at building in opportunities to provide formal feedback, unfortunately, many people honor these milestones as the only place, time, and mode in which they will receive feedback. Because of this, many leave their review, course evaluation, or midterm feeling blindsided by the fact that they "didn't know" until that moment. Imagine the growth, development, and insight you'd have if you looked beyond specific points in time? If you are only looking for feedback at the annual performance review, the annual holiday party, or when your progress report comes out, you might be missing out on the cues that tell you how you're doing. We are all sending and receiving feedback all of the time. If you scan your environment, you'll realize that there is an abundance of information that you can use to your benefit and you'll never walk into a formal feedback session surprised again.

Myth #2: All Managers are effective at giving feedback

Just because someone has a leadership title does not mean that they are inherently effective at delivering feedback. Don't believe me? Think about the leaders that you've worked for—were all of your feedback sessions smooth? Did you ever find yourself sitting across from your leader thinking, "what is happening?" or "this is not really going well"? Or perhaps you are a leader. Have you ever left a one-on-one thinking you could have delivered that feedback better? Or perhaps you started to deliver feedback and noticed tears streaming down someone's face so you thought, "Abort mission, abort mission!" Ask any leader who has the courage to deliver feedback and they will tell you that they are all doing their best but realize that they, too, have an opportunity to improve. According to an article published by Harvard Business Review (2017), they conducted a survey of 7,631 people, and 44% agreed that giving negative feedback was stressful or difficult. Twenty-one percent admitted that they avoid giving negative feedback altogether. According to Gallup (2018), only 14.5% of managers strongly agree that they are effective at giving feedback. If you happen to be in the 14.5%, good for you! But I'd challenge you to ask your team for feedback, just to be sure.

Myth #3: Feedback only comes from people in positions of power

In a world based on hierarchy, it's no surprise that many believe that feedback only comes from the top down or from people in positions of power. Employees look to their leaders, leaders look to their leaders. Students look to their teachers, teachers look to their deans. Children look to their parents and parents look to their parents. Athletes look to their coach and coaches look to the referees. Church members look to their deacons and deacons look to their pastors. While those in authority are often charged with our growth and development and typically have a responsibility to provide us with feedback, there are other sources you can explore to learn valuable insight from a different vantage point. Feedback can come from anyone—your peers, your children, your students, your employees, pretty much anyone who has seen you in action. When traditional feedback sources are lacking, looking to these additional sources will ensure your growth does not stagnate due to a lack of feedback. I am sure these additional sources will have some feedback that you might be able to leverage.

Myth #4: Feedback is explicitly stated

I know we've already addressed this, but it is important to call it out again as a myth that people must work through. Have you ever heard the phrase, "out of sight, out of mind"? I think that is how people feel about feedback. It has to be brought to their attention in a direct conversation in order for it to be feedback. They are listening for the phrase "This is feedback" in order to identify that feedback is right in front of them. The reality is, that phrase is rarely said and often times, feedback is more about what is not stated versus what is stated. You must be able to read in between the lines to understand the nuances of the information in front of you. You must have excellent self-awareness and social awareness to really be able to pick up on information you can use to support your growth.

Myth #5: Feedback is always negative

Most people understand that feedback is necessary for growth. Unfortunately, many people believe that the only way one can grow is to focus on their inadequacies and not their strengths. This might be why many people have a fear of feedback and feel cautious and anxious when they believe they will receive feedback. Feedback is not meant to focus only on where you can improve. I do think that it becomes difficult to listen if the entire conversation is focused on where you're falling short. Having a strengths-based conversation can open the hearts and minds of the individuals so that they can grow from both their strengths and think about how to leverage that strength to advance the opportunity that is shared. So, while many may have experienced feedback conversations that were focused on your deficits, know that is not the sole intent of feedback. Aristotle said, "We are what we repeatedly do. Excellence is not an act, but a habit." A big part of the growth process is getting feedback on what is working well and bringing those behaviors and skills to the forefront so that you can consciously repeat and reinforce those behaviors.

Myth #6: People do not want feedback

Some people do not provide others with feedback simply because they believe that people do not want it. According to Office Vibe (2020), 65% of employees said they wanted more feedback. So, here's a little feedback for all of those withholding feedback: quit holding out. The demand for feedback is there, but the supply is low, which means we have a lot of people who are not getting what they need to develop the confidence and competence to live out their purpose. So, when's the last time you gave someone feedback? If you have any millennials in your life, the demand for feedback is much greater. Forty-two percent of millennials say they want feedback every week (Office Vibe, 2020). The second you think, they don't want this feedback, think again.

Myth #7: The majority of people prefer positive feedback

According to Office Vibe, 82% of employees really appreciate receiving feedback regardless if it is positive or negative. In a survey of 900 global employees where they were asked if they would rather hear positive feedback about their performance or suggestions for improvement, 57% of respondents stated that they prefer corrective (negative/constructive) feedback, and only 43% stated that they prefer praise or recognition (Harvard Business Review, 2014). In short, people care more about how they can improve than hearing "good job." I know it might be easier to give positive feedback, but it is the constructive feedback that helps people close the gap between their actual and desired performance goals.

Myth #8: It's just feedback; it's not that serious

I am sorry to have to break it to you, but feedback is indeed a big deal. I surveyed a few people in my network and found out that 70% of respondents had either cried or felt depressed after receiving feedback at least once in their lives. So yes, it's that serious. Being careless with your feedback can have serious impacts on an individual's mental and emotional well-being. The recipients can be your peers, your children, your students, your spouse, your employees, or maybe even you.

Myth #9: You have to wait for feedback

Soliciting feedback on your own is a powerful but underutilized superpower. Is there an area that you have been developing but you're not sure if it's showing up in your interactions with others? Ask! Asking direct questions like, "What did you think of the activity I added?" or "What's one thing I can do to improve my ability to x?" can have a direct impact on your growth. Believe it or not, many are apprehensive about giving feedback, so by asking for feedback yourself, you take charge of your growth by getting the information you need. Social learning is a great way to grab feedback that was intended for someone else so that you can grow as well. For example, watch how people respond to others when they are doing a task, noticing what engages them or what disengages them. You can learn simply through the experiences of others by absorbing information and thinking about how you might apply that information to your own personal experiences. You can take charge of your growth by asking the sender to tell you what is working well so that you begin to develop a balanced mindset when it comes to your feedback experience.

Myth #10: Feedback is a skill you only need at work

When the word "feedback" is mentioned, the context and image that usually comes to mind first is the workplace. Yes, feedback happens in the workplace, but that is not the only place that it happens. Feedback is a skill that you need beyond the workplace because it happens anywhere there are social interactions and an exchange of information. Feedback is happening on playgrounds across the world as children try to navigate the complex process of fitting in and making friends. Imagine our children trying to confidently deliver feedback to a bully or process a feeling of rejection when they were not picked to play kickball during recess. Think about all of the feedback you encounter with the social media comments and posts that trigger an emotional response when people espouse beliefs and perspectives that are contrary to yours. Think about the feedback conversations you have to navigate when someone has violated your trust as you try to communicate your boundaries with your spouse, friends, or family. Think about the feedback you experience at church when you're trying to organize a program and everyone has a different opinion on what you should do. Think about the feedback you give your children when they have all A's and a C on their report card. Feedback is a skill you need everywhere.

There are clearly many myths floating around about feedback that are simply untrue. I believe that many struggle with the concept of feedback because we have not dedicated enough time or energy toward developing strong feedback muscles. Feedback muscle refers to the mental and emotional strength and agility required to handle feedback. If your feedback muscles are weak, you will not have the skills necessary to get the most out of every feedback experience. Feedback has been given to us since the day we were born but we never were given formal opportunities to figure out how to use it successfully unless you identify it as an opportunity for yourself. This book will walk you through how to strengthen your feedback muscles so that you create space to unlock your potential as well as the potential of others.

Constructive vs. Destructive Feedback

When developing your understanding of feedback, it is important that we reflect on the different types of feedback we may receive. Over the course of my life, I have experienced a lot of feedback, some that are dream-builders and some that are dream-killers, which is why I really wanted to write this book. I was raised believing the Biblical Scripture, Proverbs 18:21: "Death and life are in the power of the tongue." To me, this Scripture calls to our attention the power of our words and the responsibility we have to use our words wisely. I believe that you can speak positivity over someone's life or we can limit their potential all by the words that we say. As the old adage goes, "To whom much is given, much is required." With that in mind, I believe we have a social and ethical responsibility to provide people with constructive feedback and not destructive feedback.

During college, I competed in Track and Field. It was such an incredible experience competing against some of the best athletes in the nation. I was fortunate to have a pretty successful first year, winning both the Indoor and Outdoor Championships in the Long Jump. I was elated! I couldn't believe that I had achieved those personal goals. The following year, I suffered an injury, a torn hamstring. It was the worst pain I had ever felt. It completely derailed my career and hopes of pursuing the Olympic Trials one day. The rehabilitation was brutal, but I eventually worked my way back out to the field. I recall riding the charter bus to the meet with my headphones on and looking out the window. I wasn't in the mood for music but I left my headphones on my head so that it could prevent anyone from engaging with me. I was nervous, trying to get in the zone. If I were honest, I was trying to give myself a pep talk. I had lost a few meets before going to this one, so I wasn't feeling really good about myself. Then I overheard a teammate say, "Look at her, she's washed up, she's a has-been." My eyes began to tear up; it was like something sharp just stabbed me in my chest—or back, for that matter. He didn't know that I heard him, but I played that comment over and over in my head for the entire two-hour ride. I am proud to say that I channeled my anger and actually won the long jump that day. His comment became the wind beneath my wings that propelled me to success. I remember looking at him right after they announced my win to see if he had anything to say. He didn't. Here I am nearly twenty years later and I still remember his every word, every emotion, and every thought that ran through my mind.

There is a fine line between constructive and destructive feedback. Constructive feedback is feedback that is focused on growth and overall development. It is insight that focused on personal development and improvement. Destructive feedback is feedback that is meant to put someone in their place, attack or break them down or crush the human spirit. Here are some guidelines to help you gauge whether feedback is constructive or destructive:

Constructive Feedback	Destructive Feedback
Future Oriented: What is possible	Past Oriented: What happened
Focused on the behavior: Growth mindset	Focused on the person: Fixed mindset
Supportive: Stepping stones	Judgmental: Throw stones
Asset mindset: What you can do	Deficit mindset: What you cannot do

We have a responsibility to be intentional with our speech, understanding that our words have power and carry a lot of weight, especially if you are in a position of authority, influence, or senior to the person in which you are providing the feedback. Keeping feedback focused on the future gives the receiver hope about what could be. It signals that you believe that they have the ability to improve. When you provide supportive feedback, it helps them begin to think about how they might be able to improve and map out clear steps for getting there. When it is judgmental, it doesn't feel as though the conversation is a stepping stone toward success but that you're throwing stones, and that can hurt both mentally and emotionally.

If you want a guaranteed way to make someone feel as though they don't belong, focus on delivering destructive feedback. When you provide destructive feedback, it feels very personal and can make people withdraw from the conversation or relationship altogether. It can be painful and can also become a form of bullying. It can create a very demotivating atmosphere and impact their overall performance, self-esteem, sense of worth, and belonging. We all have an innate desire to belong to something and mean something to someone. Belonging is all about feeling accepted, respected, and valued. When feedback is delivered poorly, we run the risk of people feeling excluded, disrespected, or devalued. Maslow's hierarchy also states that self-esteem and self-actualization cannot be fully developed or achieved until people feel a sense of belonging (Business Balls, 2019). That in and of itself is why we have to be very thoughtful and intentional about feedback at home, in the workplace, in school, and on the field. If people do not feel as though they belong, they will not bring their full authentic selves to interactions and they're apt to hold onto ideas, or isolate themselves, which can impact their relationships and overall quality of life.

I remember the day that I received some pretty destructive feedback. It is a day I will never forget. Ironically, we were at a team-building event off-site, hoping to foster deeper connections and relationships among the team. While on a break, I approached my supervisor to get their perspective on the workshop and to share some of my own. During our conversation, my supervisor somehow managed to squeak in the phrase, "You are the most insecure person I have ever met. You walk around here in your suits like you've got it altogether but you don't." Wow, so much for fostering connections and building stronger relationships. The facilitator rang the bell and the workshop resumed before I could even respond. Quite honestly, I am glad the bell chimed right when it did, because I honestly did not know what to say. I was in complete shock. That happened at about 10:00 a.m. The workshop went until 4:30 p.m. On a scale of 0-10, how engaged do you think I was for the rest of the workshop? It was a zero. My ego was triggered; her feedback was personal, very personal. It was a judgment of my character and completely focused on what she thought I lacked. Instead of building trust in the workshop, I was focused on building an emotional wall. Yes, I'll admit it, I was in my feelings. Sitting through that training and trying to participate and be present was extremely challenging and uncomfortable for me and everyone else who was there, I am sure. If I were honest, it really stuck with me for a while, and I noticed a decline in my performance, relationships, and my overall joy.

In short, feedback is information that gives you insights into how someone perceives someone or something. Whether you are the one delivering the feedback or receiving the feedback, it is important that we handle this information with care. It has the power to influence our thoughts, feelings, behaviors, performance, and relationships. As you navigate this book, hold with you the notion and the belief that you have the ability to make a positive contribution to the development of others. And make the commitment that you will always speak life over others.

CHAPTER TWO

The Feedback Ecosystem

"Continuous delivery without continuous feedback is very, very dangerous."—Colin Humphreys

Feedback increases engagement, personal and professional growth, and overall productivity. With feedback, we have additional insight which affords us the opportunity to transform, self-correct, and position oneself for a better performance, better relationship, and more importantly, a better future. This insight is invaluable and can be one of the greatest gifts you ever receive if it is given to you, and you have the awareness, skills, and desire to leverage it. It's a tool we all have at our disposal, but unfortunately, it goes underutilized year after year. Colin Humphreys once stated, "Continuous delivery without continuous feedback is very, very dangerous." If you are delivering a product, service, project, task, assignments, or anything continuously without feedback, you are engaging in high-risk behavior. You have no idea how you're performing until you receive feedback.

You want to be thoughtful about the words you use when sending feedback, but none of that matters if you do not take the time to cultivate an environment that supports the feedback experience. In order for the feedback experience to be positive, there are several items that must be present in the Feedback Ecosystem. The Feedback Ecosystem is the environment in which people interact and exchange information, the environment in which feedback occurs. This can also be referred to as the climate or culture in which the feedback is exchanged. In order for the Feedback Ecosystem to function effectively, I believe the following conditions must be met:

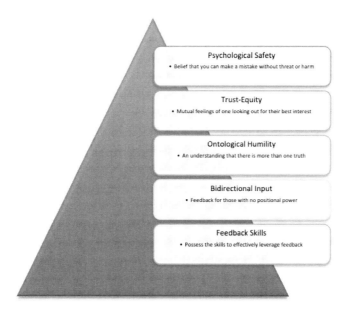

Feedback Ecosystem Need #1: Psychological Safety

It's no secret that the term "feedback" can sometimes carry a negative stigma. For many, feedback is only given when you make a mistake and is therefore correlated to punishment. Psychological safety is the belief that you won't be punished when you make a mistake (Delizonna, 2017). I believe that perfection and learning cannot occupy the same space. When you have a Feedback Ecosystem that is rich in psychological safety, people are more at ease about having conversations about mistakes. Mistakes become socially acceptable in the ecosystem when they are considered to be a part of the learning process. When psychological safety is present, the entire energy of the feedback experience shifts from negative to positive.

Tips for building psychological safety around feedback:

1. Encourage risk-taking behavior: Get people to step out of their comfort zone, try new things, and use their voice, regardless of whether they get it right or not. Creating a climate that encourages this behavior inherently sends the signal that it's okay to make a mistake because you're trying things for the first time. It also fosters a climate of innovation and productivity and boosts team morale.

2. Recognize the attempt before the result: Create a climate where you applaud people for activating the growth process by trying something new, putting themselves out there, sharing new ideas, or for speaking up. The more you recognize their attempts, it subconsciously sends a signal that taking risks and trying new things are actions that you value. If you focus on the results first, people will become preoccupied with the fact that they did not achieve the desired results and will focus on what they lack. By focusing on the attempt, you catch the positive moments and build safety and security.

3. Pause to reflect: Create a climate where taking the time to pause and reflect what you've learned both individually and collectively is a common practice. Giving people the opportunity to share what's working and where they'd like to improve fosters self-awareness, develops agency, accountability, and ownership when it comes to personal growth. This also demonstrates your commitment to the learning and growth process.

4. Encourage risk-taking behavior again: Demonstrate that you are okay with people making mistakes and learning from them—ask them to continue to get out of their comfort zone and try again. When you tell someone to try again after they fell short of the goal, it reinforces your commitment to the effort. It also reinforces that you're a coach and a teacher and that you are willing to help them get better. It also sends the signal that you believe that they have the capacity to achieve the results you desire.

Feedback Ecosystem Need #2: Trust-Equity

Trust is the firm belief in the reliability, truth, ability, or strength of someone or something (Merriam-Webster, 2020). When you trust someone, you believe that they are looking out for your best interest and that you can count on them when you need them. When trust is lacking, people are guarded, and when you are guarded, it makes the feedback conversations very difficult to navigate. How do you behave when you're interacting with someone and you know that there is no mutual trust? How might it impact your ability to send, receive, process, or apply the feedback from the conversation? The key is to build up some trust-equity so that when it comes time for feedback conversations, no one has to question each other's motives, defend themselves, or dismiss the feedback. Both parties can assume positive intent because there is mutual belief, respect, and trust in one another's motives.

Tips for building trust-equity around feedback:

1. Connect with your people: Trust grows when relationships are authentically cultivated and maintained. Have you taken the time to cultivate an authentic connection with the individuals you plan to provide feedback to? If your relationship is transactional (focused on the task or agenda) and not transformational (focused on the person/relationship), you might find that you lack the trust-equity you need to provide constructive feedback. In order for people to trust that you are looking out for their best interest, you have to connect with them and actually know their interests. They also have to have a relationship with you where they feel connected to you. Get to know their passions, motivations, goals, and aspirations. Be willing to be vulnerable and share a bit more of who you are, your motivations, and your passions. This transparency fuels authentic connections because it humanizes the relationship. If you are able to connect your feedback to how it will help them reach their goals, people are more likely to trust your motives and be receptive to feedback in the future.

2. Transparent interactions: Can you tell when someone is holding back? Most people can tell when they are not getting the full story, context, or understanding. As such, when you think about providing feedback to people, it is important that the individual regards you as a transparent, honest, and forthcoming individual. If they feel like you say one thing and mean another, it can make the feedback exchange feel very uncomfortable for all involved. To foster transparency, get comfortable with sharing how you are feeling, what you are thinking, and where you also struggle. This helps humanize you and gives space for others to connect with you. If you appear to have a block-up, the interactions can feel very robotic…and who trusts a robot? I mean, come on!

3. Be vulnerable: When it comes to building trust around the feedback process, sometimes it's best to simply be vulnerable and ask people for feedback on yourself. This can demonstrate a commitment to personal growth and further model the intent and purpose of feedback. If you are willing to be vulnerable and give the person the opportunity to tell you how you might get better, they might grow to trust the feedback process and build that trust-equity you need to better support them as well. In addition, it sends a signal that their voice and perspective are important, which is incredibly invaluable to the feedback process overall. Be sure to do the work to prepare yourself to receive feedback so that you can model it in a positive way. If you shut down or get defensive, it will diminish any trust-equity you might have built up over time.

4. Demonstrate kindness: People simply want to be respected, accepted, and valued. It is important that people are treated with respect, regardless of their position, experience, background, or ideas. Be kind. Be nice. Be compassionate. Be personable. You can give constructive feedback without making a person feel devalued. I once read a quote by an unknown author that said, "Leave a mark, not a scar." That is the goal. They should be motivated and not deflated.

Feedback Ecosystem Need #3: Ontological Humility

Ontological humility is the acknowledgment that the truth does not lie with you alone and that others have equally valid perspectives that should be heard and considered (Kofman, 2006). When you have an ecosystem where there is no hierarchy to consider with regard to perspective taking, this can create a very healthy environment. When there is a culture of ontological humility, one's perspective does not supersede another, but rather, all perspectives are needed to have a deeper understanding of the truth. When this is applied to feedback, this creates healthy dialogue between the sender and receiver and makes delivering feedback a less stressful experience. You are able to approach it with a spirit of curiosity instead of a spirit that feels more accusatory, keeping you in a space of inquiry and exploration which works much better for the receiver.

Tips for building ontological humility around feedback:

1. Ask for their perspective before sharing yours: Seeing a situation through the lens of another is a great way to stay humble. Hearing their perspective helps you develop empathy and possibly uncover potential influencers on the outcome that you had not yet explored. Asking for their opinion first creates space for one's authentic voice and perspective to be shared. Even though you are giving someone feedback, be prepared to learn from them as well. They may share insights, needs, challenges, or concerns that you never knew. Go into your feedback session with a mindset that says, "I have something I can learn from this discussion." This will help you to remain humble and open to different perspectives. Oftentimes, the person of influence shares their opinion and others simply agree because they are afraid to share if their opinion differs.

Feedback blocking is when someone is unwilling to have a two-way feedback exchange. It is when feedback is one-directional and not bidirectional. Giving the feedback recipient the opportunity to add their input is a critical part of the feedback process. It allows them to share their understanding of the behavior displayed and why they decided to do the things that were observed. Remember, you do not have all of the data until you have their insight as well. You can learn a great deal about your feedback recipient by listening to their rationale. This will also help you identify what potential solutions should be explored to best support their development. When they are a part of your feedback discussion, this helps to gain their buy-in to the solutions and action steps.

2. **Balance** questions and statements: Ask questions 80% of the time and make statements 20% of the time. Making this a general practice will help you stay in a state of inquiry. This helps to keep you in a space of listening and broadening your understanding about the situation you wanted to discuss. Intentionally scaling back your perspective to make space for others on a continuous basis can foster a climate where people are used to sharing their thoughts and opinions, regardless of the topic at hand. This will help demonstrate that all voices and opinions are valuable and that just because you are in a position of influence, your opinion is not the only perspective worth hearing.

Feedback Ecosystem Need #4: Bidirectional feedback

Often times, feedback is seen as one-directional which carries the stigma that only individuals who lead others can provide feedback. To create an environment where growth and continuous development is not just a saying but a practice that is embraced by all, it is important to take the lid off of feedback and make it bidirectional. That is, feedback can flow from top to bottom and from bottom to top.

Tips for facilitating bidirectional feedback:

1. Ask for feedback about your leadership from those without positional power: Demonstrate a willingness to develop, regardless of your positional power. This can be formal such as soliciting during performance reviews or as informal as asking what can you do to improve in a one-to-one setting.

2. Request input about projects from those without positional power: Demonstrate a commitment to ontological humility and feedback by asking for feedback on other subjects such as projects, process improvements, etc. These small but powerful behaviors will signal that feedback is a desired part of the culture.

Feedback Ecosystem Need #5: Feedback Skills

This one may seem like a no-brainer, but it is important to discuss the need for feedback skills. In order for the ecosystem to thrive, every member of the ecosystem, regardless of position, power or privilege, must develop their ability to deliver, receive, process, and apply feedback. If the members of the community do not have adequate training, we will never be able to build psychological safety, trust-equity, ontological humility, or bidirectional feedback. Instead, it will erode each of those items away and create an environment where people are more likely to hoard feedback, become defensive, withdraw, gossip, or end relationships altogether. You must be willing to invest the time and energy into your development and the development of members so that you can foster an environment where people can thrive.

Have you ever sat with a group of people only to feel the collective tension begin to rise when someone challenged their point of view? Have you seen people go from happy to angry because someone could not handle the feedback on their presentations, projects, or behaviors? It's really difficult to watch. The most uncomfortable thing to watch is a well-intentioned person struggle to give constructive criticism. The most disheartening thing to witness is the recipient walk away believing that they are not worthy, intelligent, or valued. I know there are a lot of variables that go into this experience (timing, content, delivery, history), but at the most basic level, we haven't even given most of us a chance to be successful. We have to ensure that everyone has these skills, not just those with the power to access this knowledge.

Tips for building feedback skills:

a. Knowledge and Mindset: The best way to develop knowledge is by first starting with reading. I hope this book gives you the foundation you need to develop a shared language and understanding of feedback so that it can activate the skill-building process. Developing personal knowledge about what it is, how it works, and where your knowledge gaps lie can be a powerful starting place. Don't hoard the knowledge; be sure to share it with others. Give them the gift of knowledge by gifting them this book as a great foundation for increasing their knowledge and self-awareness.

b. Skills: To develop skills, it takes intentional and concentrated practice. Take advantage of our skill-building courses at www.feedbackmentality.com to take your knowledge and transfer it into a skill that can build a strong Feedback Mentality. Recommended Sentence: Encourage a healthy environment where people are challenged to give, receive, process, and apply feedback on an ongoing basis.

It is important that we think about the ecosystem in which feedback lives. We must have psychological safety, trust-equity, ontological humility, bidirectional input, and strong feedback skills in our ecosystem in order to truly harness the power of feedback. It is our hope that you have a better understanding of the many influences to the feedback experience and feel empowered to enact change.

Reflection Questions

1. Which elements of the ecosystem are present in the communities in which you interact? How do you know?

2. Which elements of the ecosystem are missing? How do you know?

3. What will you do to improve the health of your feedback ecosystem?

4. How will you know when you are successful?

CHAPTER THREE

Feedback Stories

"When we deny our stories, they define us. When we own our stories, we get to create a brave new ending." —Brene Brown

Think about where you are at this very moment. Look around the room, feel the chair that holds you up, feel your heart pulsating throughout your body, take in the air and everything that sustains you. Plant your feet firmly on the ground. You are here. Think about where you are. How did you get here? There was a series of people, experiences, and decisions that shaped who you are, how you feel, and who you've become. It is feedback that helps us to understand the phenomenon of our journey. It is the feedback that shapes our thoughts, our thoughts becoming our narratives, and our narratives becoming the stories we tell ourselves, the stories we tell others, and ultimately, they becomes the story of our lives.

Libby Bray once said, "There's no greater power on earth than story." The stories we watch on television can take us on an emotional journey full of highs and lows, but there's always a lesson we can take from it. There are powerful stories and narratives that you have been playing in your mind that are guiding you to the next chapter of your life. I asked a few of my colleagues to share some of their feedback stories in hopes that you can understand the power of feedback from the lens of others. Reflect on these short stories and see what you might take into your own feedback experience.

Personal Feedback Story #1: Simone Davis, Founder/Owner, An Eye 4 Art, LLC

Feedback is inevitable! I have received solicited, unsolicited, biased, unbiased, hurtful, and helpful feedback in my personal and professional life, but before delving into how I process feedback, allow me to digress and paint the picture of what incident created that paradigm shift in my life.

As a young woman growing up in the Caribbean, the fifth child of seven, I struggled to define who I was as an individual, inherently different from my siblings. I was not the smartest, definitely the loudest, always the risk-taker and a forever dreamer.

In high school, I received THE feedback that was the defining moment for me. I was told that I would NEVER amount to anything. That was all that was said to me, a fourteen-year-old at the time, by my Catholic school nun with no context. I was devastated! As a teen struggling to find my voice and identity, I felt powerless and if I'm to be candid, I shrunk a little. I was already an awkward teen who did not know who she was or what she wanted to become when she grew up, but I unequivocally knew that I did not want to be a NOTHING.

I struggled with accepting this unsolicited, what seemed at the time, hurtful feedback from an educator who spent such a small fraction of time in a classroom with me. Someone who was to encourage and uplift, not to tear down. What was her motive? I do know that I lost trust in my educators. I remember thinking, *what crystal ball were you peering into that you could predict my future?*

At the time of that life-changing feedback, I didn't know how to ask for examples of specific behavioral patterns that I exhibited. In fact, I'm fairly sure I did not ask questions or retaliated, as that was unbecoming of a young person to speak back to or question an authoritarian figure.

As I progressed through high school for the next two and a half years, my self-worth dwindled, and doubt kicked in. I had so many questions about that encounter but didn't know how to effectively deal with it. My family was supportive of whatever I did, but deep inside, I had a sense that they too may have had the same thoughts about my future. I grew defensive about every feedback I received because it all felt very personal.

I was a late bloomer. While my friends went off to business school and colleges, I entered the workforce at eighteen and spent the next six years trying to find myself and my value, still with very little understanding of how to quell my internalized fears associated with any feedback.

In the years to follow, I developed a love of travel which piqued my cultural curiosity and openness toward others. I was able to have unfiltered, raw, and uncomfortably candid conversations. It wasn't until I completed my undergraduate studies at the age of twenty-nine and became a supervisor in my first career that I truly discovered that feedback—solicited, unsolicited, biased, unbiased, hurtful or helpful—if taken with a grain of salt and deep self-reflection to identify patterns of unproductivity, would help me grow and set my intentions for whom I wanted to become and what I wanted to achieve.

I will never know why I was given that feedback in high school, but over the course of my life, I became empowered by it. It has framed my passion for serving, coaching, and helping others in an empathetic and nonjudgmental way. I became intentional about how I would give feedback to others. I provide specificity focused on behavioral traits that could be changed, not personal rhetoric to inflict hurt.

How to process feedback, in my opinion, is a learned behavior and should be integrated into learning at an early age to support cognitive processing for better performance and healthy outcomes, not to threaten self-esteem.

Reflection Questions:

1. What thoughts and feelings came to mind as you read this story?

2. What will you take from this story that can assist you on your feedback journey?

Personal Feedback Story #2: Dr. Cecil Wright, Co-Founder, AimHigh Empowerment Institutes

Facts are important, numbers tell a story, but the most important thing you can do in giving feedback is leaning in. I came to that conclusion only after a conversation with my uncle a few years ago. After working forty-two years in the public sector, listening to thousands of civilian concerns, and fighting government bureaucracies, one would think that the lessons learned from giving feedback would center around getting to the facts. I asked him, "Should I look for a new career opportunity because I was overlooked for a very important promotion?" He responded by stopping the car, turning off the radio, and stepping out of the car. Now in the shade, protected from the blistering heat, he proceeded to sit on an outdoor bench and said, "Tell me more." His forty-two years of giving feedback was in full display. To respond to my question, he came to a complete stop, removed every distraction from around him, listened thoroughly, then responded. He was leaning in and changing his position.

I ultimately took his advice and applied for a new position in a different company and "tadah!" I got the job! This new position was ideal. The organization needed a mid-level manager with strong connections to the industry, strong connections to the community, and someone who could help re-energize the organization's culture in the locations that they were struggling in. I had no doubt that I was the man for the job and I immediately went to work. I met with my direct reports weekly, held interdepartmental meetings with the team, studied the data, and started working on creating a new culture. In less than six months, things began to change. At one location, staff morale increased as evidenced by a 75% reduction in tardiness and sick days and a 23% increase in revenue compared to the previous year. The other location also saw improvement in staff morale by 53% with reduced tardiness but remained flat in other areas. However, the greater challenge for each location was much more than personnel. Many services that would drive the location revenue were not available at those locations but the data showed that my team was doing an excellent job with what they had and more importantly, attitudes were being changed. I felt that at the core of this organization's success would be developing a group of people who love what they do and to help them find their purpose.

I was there for about a year when I received a phone call from my direct supervisor asking when I would be in their location.

I responded that I would be there for a meeting the next day so it was requested that I swing by their office. On my visit the next day, I made plans to swing by immediately after my meeting. Upon approaching the office, I was waved in. I was barely seated when the conversation began with, "How are you?" After I responded, the next thing I heard was, "You did not get the numbers we were expecting in one location and I will be promoting someone else to take over that location." My supervisor further continued with, "I know you are doing a good job but now that you have only one location, you need to hit it out of the park." The conversation ended with, "I know you can do it. I have no doubt you will." I did not have time to process anything. I did not know how to respond. I was totally blindsided because there was no prior indication that this was coming.

I tried to muster a response while simultaneously trying to process what just happened. My supervisor asked if I understood; I said yes because it was the easiest thing to stay. I left the room and all I could remember is the shuffling of papers on the desk, the tone, the quickness of the statement, and a fainting feeling in my stomach. The entire experience left me feeling deflated, defeated, and demoralized.

Reflection Questions:

1. What thoughts and feelings came to mind as you read this story?

2. What will you take from this story that can assist you on your feedback journey?

Personal Feedback Story #3: Cameron Thomas of Cameron Thomas Voiceovers.com

I recall hearing someone mention that a good leader makes them feel important. And feedback is how you do it. Having worked in many different areas—the military, higher education, weather forecasting, broadcasting, freelance voiceovers—I have given and received feedback in all sorts of ways. But it was during my time as a drummer in a band that the feedback I received had the most impact.

During a casual dinner with some bandmates, the singer started talking about my playing style. He continued about how my drumming style and technique complemented the band. It was the most flattering feedback I have ever received. After twenty-five years of playing, it reinforced everything that I read, absorbed, practiced, and applied to playing drums...and most importantly, how it impacted the band as a whole. It made me feel…important.

Sure, the feedback was fantastic, but *how* it was delivered was the key for me as well. It was intentional but impromptu.

Purposeful but casual. Just organic and genuine—and, in front of the rest of the band. That type of informal, reinforcing feedback had a huge impact on me and is how I want to provide feedback to others.

Part of my approach was also shaped by the military. We had annual performance evaluations and only a couple of formal feedback sessions a year, so any feedback outside of that was informal—unless you really screwed up and got called on the carpet! And if there was time for feedback outside of that, it was for a good butt-chewing. If you messed up, you took it, and got back to the mission. No need to be called on the carpet. That informal style was quick and impactful. Get it? Got it? Good!

And how many times have you heard of managers providing feedback only when it's negative. Get called to the office? Uh-oh, that's not good. Why is "going to the office" always a negative thing? So, when it came to working as a team lead at an online university, I wanted to put it all together to ensure that I provided intentional, informal, and frequent reinforcing feedback as much as possible.

When I performed quality assessments on customer service calls, if I heard an impressive interaction with a student, I went directly over to the advisor to offer the feedback. No need to wait for the formal written report. Just a brief mention of the action, the positive impact, a high-five, and kudos. If someone from another department assisted with an issue, I personally walked over to them to show my appreciation for their actions. No need for an email. Any time a teammate accomplished a big task or hit a goal, I just went over to them, pat them on the back with a big shout-out. No need to wait for an award. And I made it a point to do it in front of others.

Even in a formal setting of a team meeting, I made it a point to highlight a positive behavior from someone—or several—on the team in front of the whole team. Before long, we had other teammates sharing positive experiences that they observed from their teammates to reinforce the feeling of importance and contribution. Being approached by a supervisor was not something to fear, and when we offer reinforcing feedback, publicly or privately, formally or informally, people feel important. Get it? Got it? Good!

Reflection Questions:

1. What thoughts and feelings came to mind as you read this story?

2. What will you take from this story that can assist you on your feedback journey?

Personal Feedback Story #4: Margi Mejia, Strategic Human Capital Leader

In a leadership role at my new organization, both in industry and model, I received feedback through an annual LOOP survey. These surveys gave your peers and those junior to you the opportunity to provide feedback on several categories including your coaching style, value you bring, and business acumen. Surveys were to be sent by you to whomever you chose.

I decided that being a brave employee, open to feedback, I would send it out to the entire group of over forty people I worked with. I opened myself up, thinking that all feedback is a gift and I should appreciate anything people were courageous enough to share with me, despite being anonymous.

When I received my survey results, I immediately opened up the document, anxious for the stories they would tell. While there were several categories to review, I found myself focusing on those that rated, in my eyes, lower than I would have anticipated. I actually found myself having a physical reaction, feeling nauseous and actually dreading my feedback session with my coach, who was also my senior manager.

While she was attempting to focus on the positives, I heard myself disregarding her and bringing up areas I felt were short-comings. She finally stopped me and shared her own results, where she, too, had areas of opportunity to improve. She realized that I needed someone to acknowledge my areas of opportunity before I could hear any of the areas that I was strong in. I needed to create a path for improvement before I could let myself acknowledge that there were areas where I might actually be able to support others.

What I learned was that in order for me to accept the feedback as the "gifts" they were, I first needed time, then needed to address growth opportunities, and finally, acceptance that despite having some shortcomings, I still had strengths to be leveraged.

This was the first time in a long time I had been with both an organization and a coach/manager who allowed me the chance to receive feedback purely with the intent for growth. Because this was such a new and foreign concept, I did not know what to do with it as first. Now, I can take this moment of great discomfort and use it as an example as I coach others.

I have always quoted to others, "Is it true? Is it kind? Is it necessary?" This experience gave me the opportunity to really live the "necessity" of feedback. Finally, I feel completely honest when I say, "I'm open to the feedback!"

Reflection Questions:

1. What thoughts and feelings came to mind as you read this story?

2. What will you take from this story that can assist you on your feedback journey?

Now that you've had the time to reflect on the feedback stories of others, it can be a powerful exercise to reflect on the feedback stories you've accumulated over the course of your life. Reflecting on your own lived experience with delivering, receiving, and processing feedback can be an empowering point of introspection. It will help you tap into the empathy needed to approach the feedback experience with humanity.

Reflection Questions:

1. What is the most difficult piece of feedback you have ever received?

2. What was the most rewarding feedback you've ever received?

3. How have those experiences helped to shape who you've become?

4. How do you want people to feel when you deliver feed back to them?

5. What do you need to learn, do, say, or believe in order to make that a reality?

CHAPTER FOUR

Understanding Your Feedback Mentality

"There is no failure. Only feedback." —Robert Allen

To fully embrace feedback, you have to have a well-constructed ecosystem but you also have to have the right mentality. Mentality is defined as "mental power or capacity; mode or way of thought" (Merriam-Webster, 2020). A Feedback Mentality is a mindset that is in relentless pursuit of your highest potential by leveraging information around you. Do you have a strong feedback mentality? This section will explore the *Four Feedback Muscles* you need to develop a resilient Feedback Mentality and explore symptoms that might indicate a more vulnerable Feedback Mentality.

Four Feedback Muscles

1. **Delivering Feedback**: The physical act of giving feedback to others.

2. **Receiving Feedback:** The physical act of receiving feedback from others.

3. **Processing Feedback**: The mental act of analyzing the internal narrative attached to feedback.

4. **Applying Feedback:** The process of prioritizing and acting on feedback.

Symptoms of a vulnerable Feedback Mentality

Symptom #1: Hoarding vs. Giving (Delivering Feedback)

It's time that we get the courage to call out our inner feedback hording tendencies and step up and deliver feedback. Willfully withholding feedback from others can be damaging. It can be an area of opportunity that could change the trajectory of their lives if they only knew that it was an opportunity. This doesn't mean going around and telling everyone you meet what you think about them, but it is an honest assessment of whether or not you should provide constructive feedback for their betterment. If you are in a position of authority and are responsible for the growth and development of others, you have a social and ethical responsibility to give both positive and developmental feedback.

What are some of the reasons why you tend to hoard instead of give feedback? Is it skill or will? If it's skill, we'll show you how to develop those skills shortly, but if it's will, that is something that you own. If you do not have the will or desire to give others feedback, you have to really ask yourself if you should be in the position that you are in and whether or not you value the relationship that is in need of the feedback. We can help you build the courage and skill to deliver feedback, but the will to give feedback is something only you can own and cultivate.

Symptom #2: Freestyling vs. Preparing (Delivering Feedback)

When I was little, the kids in our neighborhood would make mixed tapes of our favorite songs and play them until the tape literally broke. We loved music—it was like every song had meaning and was the soundtrack of our childhood. One of the things we used to do was a freestyle contest. We'd play the instrumental and everyone would have a chance to come up with their own lyrics and the group would vote for the best freestyle. I used to fumble every time, never making it through the first two bars. I couldn't handle the pressure, it was too much to process. I buckled every time. But if you asked me to come prepared with a few bars, I could handle it, no problem.

Some people are great at doing things on the fly, but you should really do a bit of preparation when it comes to delivering feedback. This is not to say that you shouldn't give feedback in the moment, it just means you want to take the time to be clear about what behavior you want to address and why before giving the feedback. Taking the time to prepare and think intentionally about what feedback you plan to give is a healthy mindset to have. It gives you the space and time to decide the best method, timing, and delivery so that you can maximize effectiveness. Taking the time to prepare can also prove beneficial if the feedback you are about to deliver triggers an emotional response. When you are triggered emotionally, you might find that you are more apt to say things that you don't mean or things that can be damaging to the relationship. Pausing to prepare will ensure that you've thought through the best approach possible.

Symptom #3: Labeling vs. Learning (Receiving Feedback)

Labels are a part of our everyday life. If you look around my kitchen, you will find labels everywhere. The sugar, the flour, the salt and pepper all have clearly printed labels across the front of their containers. Labels help to unmistakably identify what something is. I mean, who would want to put a heap of flour in their oatmeal? Thank goodness for labels. There are other items in my kitchen that do not have printed labels but items I have ascribed mental labels to. For example, if you open up my pantry, I have categorized my snacks by kids snacks, adult snacks, healthy snacks, and guilty pleasure snacks. Hey, don't judge me—a good snack is defined by the details. These labels give me the opportunity to make quick decisions about what I want to eat and anticipate the pros and cons of eating it.

Labeling is not restricted to the kitchen. It can be used when referencing people, places, or things. It becomes a quick description that holds a narrative that can shape how you interact with something or someone. Being able to quickly identify something as safe or harmful, good or bad can, in many cases, be lifesaving. It's a tool we use to make sense of the world. Unfortunately, there is not a perfect science to labeling, so you can inaccurately label something or someone which can also have a negative outcome for you or the person, place, or thing.

When it comes to feedback, labeling can be the sign of an unhealthy feedback mentality. Labeling in this context is when one is focused on attributing negative characteristics to the individual delivering the feedback in an effort to dismiss or minimize the value of the feedback. If you find yourself attributing a negative label to those who give you feedback, the negative emotions that come with that label may cloud your ability to "hear" the feedback and hear it in an unbiased or unemotional manner. Labeling someone "stupid" or "incompetent" does not create a space for you to learn from the feedback that is given. It also does not put you in the right mental state to deliver feedback either. Labels typically carry a story and stories usually have emotions, and if the label is emotionally charged enough, your rational brain might not even be "online" to begin to find learning opportunities for growth from the feedback.

Sometimes labels are attributed before the feedback is given or in the middle of receiving feedback. Sometimes, the way people deliver the feedback can trigger the labeling process. Their tone or delivery style might make you label them as "bad" or "rude," "insensitive," "mean," "bully," or other choice words I wouldn't dare say aloud, let alone write in print. Once we find ourselves labeling the messenger, we can prevent ourselves from simply hearing the message.

Symptom #4: Leaning in vs. Leaning out (Receiving Feedback)

Albert Mehrabian is known for the 7-55-38 rule (Businessballs, 2019). This rule is the breakdown of human communication: 7 percent spoken words, 38 percent tone of voice, and 55 percent body language. Think about the body language you display when you are speaking to someone you are interested in. Now, contrast that to the body language you display when you are not "feeling it." When you are leaning in during a feedback session, you are probably displaying interest, curiosity, and a desire to understand. It's important to note that there's a difference between leaning in and lunging in, so be mindful of the speed at which you lean in and the energy with which you do it as well. When you are leaning out, you might be sending off the signal that you're disinterested or in disagreement with the feedback.

When you display defensive posture, it triggers the person's defense mechanism as well. This can really make the feedback experience difficult as the brain decides whether or not to go into fight, flight, or freeze mode. If both parties are triggered and feel as though they need to defend themselves from a potential attack, this becomes an argument, not a healthy feedback session.

Symptom #5: Ruminating vs. Problem-Solving (Processing Feedback)

It is natural to reflect on the negative feedback that you receive or an event that occurs. When done well, reflection helps you unlock new bits of information that will help you identify ways to solve a problem. An unhealthy form of self-reflection is called rumination. Rumination is characterized by repetitive and persistent evaluation of the meaning, causes, and consequences of one's emotional state and personal concerns (Nolen-Hoeksema, Wisco, and Lyubomirsky, 2008). In the moment, replaying the feedback over and over may feel like a productive use of time, but replaying painful events and feedback over and over often increases negative affect and impairs problem solving (Lyubomirsky, 1995).

Oprah Winfrey once said, "I know for sure that what we dwell on is who we become." I know plenty of people who ruminate from time to time. It starts off as a simply replay of events and then before you know it, they are locked in a vicious cycle playing back the entire conversation word for word and analyzing the tone of the feedback, the body language of the sender, the location of the feedback, the context of the feedback, the inference of the feedback, and more. They can go from 0 to 100 in their mind and their emotional state changes right along with it. By the time they stop ruminating, they are usually exhausted and feel down and depressed with no resolution in sight. If we become what we dwell on, we have to switch from admiring the problem to solving the problem if we want to have a healthy relationship with feedback and a positive outcome.

Symptom #6: Absorbing vs. Filtering (Processing Feedback)

No one is perfect, so we all rely on the feedback loop from others to describe the gap between our intended behaviors and perception of our behaviors so that we can achieve our desired results. There is a fine line between being open to feedback and absorbing every piece of information you come into contact with. I know we've all been taught to "be a sponge," but what if a sponge mentality was actually preventing you from living out your full potential? A sponge mentality is the mindset of holding onto constructive feedback for an indefinite amount of time. A sponge can only hold so much before it starts to become full and begin to overflow, cross-contaminating everything it touches. You can hold onto so much feedback that you do not have enough space to do anything with it. All of the negative bits of information just take up space in your mind and begin to impact all of your interactions.

Oprah talks about suffering from "disease to please" which is the desire to make everyone happy. I think that is why many hold onto everyone's feedback. It's like there's a desire to do everything that everyone else wants for the sake of peace and making every-one else happy. But the reality is, acting on feedback should be for you, not for them. It's important that you get better at listening to the feedback and filtering through what you receive so that you can have a more intentional, strategic, and healthy approach to feedback.

Symptom #7: Reacting vs. Responding (Applying Feedback)

When it comes to feedback, it is important to think about whether you are reacting or responding to the feedback provided. Reacting to feedback can make people feel good in the moment because it typically involves quickly implementing actions that will address the feedback. Sometimes the reaction is so quick that it feels subconscious and automatic. When we react to feedback, it almost operates like a defense mechanism, trying to reduce the pain. When we react to feedback, it often pleases the sender in the moment by demonstrating our willingness to improve and further avoid discussions about the area identified. Is that the way we want to live? We should not be reacting to every single piece of feedback we encounter. If we do, we run the risk of quickly implementing behaviors for the sake of checking off boxes. With this reaction, you are not really engaging in behavior change and long-term growth.

If you want a healthy feedback mentality, the focus must be on responding to feedback versus reacting to feedback. Responding involves engaging the heart and head in an analysis of what the best action should be, looking at all angles of the feedback, and being thoughtful about what to do with it. It may take a bit longer to come up with a plan, but the long-term impact will be beneficial to both the sender and receiver.

Symptom #8: Neglecting vs. Prioritizing (Applying Feedback)

Have you been given feedback that you know you should address but failed to do so? Perhaps you're unsure where to start, not clear about what the feedback means, or you are simply just too overwhelmed to focus on it? If so, I completely understand. In order to get to a healthy state with your feedback, we have to develop the skills to identify what to prioritize, act on, and what can wait. Doing so will empower you to reap the benefits of the information that will take your performance, relationship, and overall growth to the next level.

There are times in which people have so much feedback that they become fatigued. Feedback fatigue occurs when one becomes mentally and emotionally overwhelmed by the opportunities to improve. When you have ten things to improve on from your manager, three things from your spouse, two things from your teacher, six things from your parents… you get the point. It can become quite the task to improve in all of those areas while still maintaining healthy self-esteem and a positive outlook. We will discuss tips for prioritizing the feedback so that the important and urgent items are addressed and not be detractors when it comes to your growth.

Building Feedback Muscle

As a child, I had a natural affinity for sports. I enjoyed basketball, softball, cross-country, and track. Well, I am not sure that I really enjoyed cross-county. I mean, who just runs for miles through hills and wicked trails for enjoyment? The truth is, cross-country was painful; all of the sports were hard, but I found that the more I practiced, it all got easier, even cross-country. I started to build runners muscle—you know, the kind of muscles that had enough strength to propel you down the hill in a full-out sprint right into the home stretch, straight to that finish like you hadn't been running for nearly thirty minutes. I loved the roar of the crowd, cheering me on, amazed at that final sprint to the finish! And I'd cross the line proud, not proud of winning—because I didn't (I was always like 50th or so out of 100), but proud that my muscles were strong enough to carry me to the end after those long, hard courses. I'll be honest, I wasn't born with runners muscle. It required intentional practice.

We are all born with vulnerable feedback muscles. They are underdeveloped until our lived experiences begin to shape how we respond. Reflect on the descriptions of vulnerabilities of feedback. Do you have the mental and emotional strength to deliver feedback, receive feedback, process, and apply feedback? Are you stronger in some areas of feedback and weaker in others?

Now that you had a chance to review the signs and symptoms, let's check the overall health of your feedback mentality so that you have the feedback you need to develop.

Feedback Muscle Check-Up

Step 1: Circle behavior that best defines how you handle critical feedback most of the time.

Resilient Feedback Mentality	Vulnerable Feedback Mentality
Hoarding (Delivering) Withholding feedback from others	Sharing (Delivering) Providing feedback to others
Freestyling (Delivering) Knee-jerk feedback delivery	Preparing (Delivering) Thoughtfully planned feedback delivery
Labeling (Receiving) Attributing negative characteristics to the sender	Learning (Receiving) Listening intently to the feedback regardless of sender
Leaning out (Receiving) Body language and position is away from sender	Leaning in (Receiving) Body language and position is towards the sender
Absorbing (Processing) Holding on to all of feedback you encounter	Filtering (Processing) Taking in feedback, learning from it and intentionally letting somethings go

Ruminating (Processing) Replaying the feedback over and over analyzing the delivery and intent	Problem Solving (Processing) Understanding the feedback and finding ways to solve the problem at hand
Reacting (Applying) Automatic/Subconscious application of the feedback	Responding (Applying) Strategic/Conscious application of the feedback
Neglecting (Applying) Not addressing the feedback given	Prioritizing (Applying) Strategically identifying what to focus on based on the feedback given

Step 2: Add up the total number of items circled and list the total below.

- The column with the largest number best describes your general tendencies toward feedback and overall mentality.

- Use this feedback to assist you with cultivating your own development as you continue through the remainder of this book.

Step 3: Review the **Resilient Mentality** column and identify which categories are your strengths.

__ Delivering Feedback

__ Receiving Feedback

__ Processing Feedback

__ Applying Feedback

Step 4: Review the **Vulnerable Mentality** column and rank which categories you should **develop** in order of priority.

__ Delivering Feedback

__ Receiving Feedback

__ Processing Feedback

__ Applying Feedback

Now that you are aware of your muscle strengths and vulnerabilities, it is time to get to work! In order to build your feedback muscle, you will have to commit to stepping out of your comfort zone a bit so that you are able to get in the practice time needed to become proficient in each of the four muscle groups. The road to development looks different for each individual. The next few chapters are dedicated to isolating each feedback muscle so that you can build strong muscles and increase your efficacy with feedback.

Reflection Questions

1. Which feedback muscle will be the most difficult to develop? Why?

2. How might you leverage your strengths to help you in this area?

3. How will you know if you're improving with feedback?

4. Who will hold you accountable to your development?

CHAPTER FIVE

Delivering Feedback

"The people who have taught me the most in my career are the ones who pointed out what I didn't see." —Sheryl Sandberg

The most stressful time of the year for me has to be the holiday season. No, it's not the decorations, the travel from house to house or the cooking that makes me stress. It's the shopping. Shopping for gifts has to be the most stressful thing in the world. Walking from aisle to aisle, trying to find the perfect gift that is meaningful and personalized to each and every person. I would always find myself wondering if they will find value in the gift, if they will appreciate the thought that went into the gift, if they understood the intent of the gift, and how they'd respond when they opened the gift. Not only was finding the right gift stressful, but making sure I wrapped it beautifully was an experience in and of itself.

The wrapping paper, the custom bow, and the beautifully written gift tag—the entire production makes a difference.

Honestly, as much as I complain about shopping for gifts, it's all worth it in the end. When I finally hand them that gift that I know they've been thinking about all year, or when I get them something that sparks or reinforces their dreams or goals… it feels so good to watch them experience it and use it for years to come. It feels good when they give you a hug or a big smile of thanks. It is those moments when you feel like all of the hustle and bustle was all worth it. But we know that isn't the outcome of every gift-giving experience. There are those times when I've given someone a meaningful gift and they break it, never use it, say they didn't want it, regift it, or just let it sit in their closet collecting dust until the next gift exchange opportunity. All that work for nothing. So many pass on giving gifts altogether or just settle for gift cards.

I am confident that you have had plenty of opportunities to give someone the gift of feedback at some point in your life. And yes, it can be just as stressful and rewarding as giving someone a gift for the holidays. You spend your time picking out the right thing to say and packaging it in a way that you hope they will receive it. You wait to see their reaction and hope it will be something that they come to use over the years. All feedback experiences have the potential to change behavior, so technically, all feedback can be life-changing. According to Gallup (2019), only 26% of employees strongly agree that the feedback they receive helps them do better work. This means 74% of employees do not feel as though feedback is helping them improve! According to Gallup (2020), only 17% of millennials report receiving meaningful feedback. This means your gift of feedback might be sitting on someone's mental shelf collecting dust or it's been discarded altogether.

Delivering feedback can be hard! If you are a leader, spouse, parent, co-worker, friend, teacher, clergy member, or coach, then I am sure you find yourself in a position where you are looked to for advice, direction, and yes, feedback. When you are in a position of influence and you hold the responsibility of helping others develop, people expect you to provide them with meaningful, honest, and genuine input on how they are doing with their personal and professional goals. But let's be honest, you hate giving constructive feedback! And many times you avoid it, because you're scared and don't want them to take it too personally, get defensive, or whip out their verbal judo and use it on you. If you are in a position where you provide others with feedback, it is important that you do it in a way that makes them feel worthy and not worthless. This chapter will help you get the most out of your feedback conversations with those you care about the most.

Human resources professional, Kevin Williams, once said, "Poorly delivered feedback can feel like a tornado in the mind." It is important that we are intentional in our delivery of feedback so that we have the right conditions for it to be heard and received. If it feels like a tornado, you can guarantee that they are not getting the message. There is a great deal of literature and research about how to deliver feedback effectively. But I believe there's an opportunity to discuss the two symptoms that indicate we might be vulnerable when delivering feedback. These two areas are where we need to focus our energy if we are to become more effective at delivering feedback:

1. Hoarding feedback: Willfully withholding feedback from others

2. Freestyling feedback: Delivering feedback without proper preparation

Are you a feedback hoarder? Are you willfully withholding feedback from others? According to Officevibe (2020), 28% of employees report that feedback is not frequent enough to help them understand how to improve. Withholding feedback is like withholding the opportunity to grow, which can prevent children, students, partners, parents, employees, athletes, supervisors, church members, business owners, and all of those who are looking to grow to remain stagnant. The reality is, not everyone has been given the opportunity to experience the power of feedback. Not everyone has been empowered with information about the past or present that they can leverage for their future.

I recall working alongside a woman who was very intelligent, compassionate, and hardworking. I remember being so impressed by all of the knowledge she had and how she exceeded her performance goals time and time again. She applied for a leadership role and did not get it. I remember her sharing that she was disappointed but that she would try again. She was optimistic so she applied again and again to any and every open leadership role available within that department function, but was never offered a leadership position.

Eventually, I changed roles and I was able to be a part of the leadership interview process. This woman's name came up again as an applicant for an open leadership role. I was surprised to hear that the panel did not believe she had the skills to lead. My only question was, "does SHE know that?" I honestly do not believe she did. I recall feeling sad that the employee had no idea that she didn't have the skills they were looking for and as such, would never grow the skills they believe she lacked. What were those skills? Did anyone work with her to build those skills? When I think about this scenario, it reminds me that feedback is powerful, for without it, people may be operating with an unknown gap that could prevent them from upward mobility, financial stability, developing purpose and meaning, and living to their full potential. Do you see why feedback is powerful?

If you are in a position of authority and are responsible for the growth and development of others, you have a social and ethical responsibility to give both positive and developmental feedback. For starters, here are a few questions to ask yourself when you feel yourself holding onto feedback:

Improve	Impact	Future	You
• Could this feedback help them improve?	• Will other people be negatively impacted if this behavior is not addressed?	• Will this feedback impact their future if they do not receive this feedback?	• Would you want to know this feedback if it were you?

Improve Question: Could this feedback help them improve?

- Think about how this feedback might support immediate opportunities for growth. How might it impact their performance if they had knowledge of this feedback?

Impact Question: Will other people be negatively impacted if this behavior is not addressed?

- Think about others who will benefit from this person having this feedback and improving their performance, relationship, or outcome.

Future Question: Will this feedback impact their future if they do not receive this feedback?

- How might this feedback play out in their lives in the long run? What are the net consequences of this behavior going unaddressed?

You Question: Would you want to know this feedback if it were you?

- If you were in this person's place, how much would you value the feedback you are holding onto? How might it make you feel if you knew someone was with holding this information?

If you answered yes to at least one of the questions, you know what you need to do. Deliver the feedback! Be brave! If you are not giving feedback when you know you should, I am going to give YOU some feedback right now: you're not meeting the expectations of your role. Your role can be parent, coach, sibling, friend, co-worker, teacher or supervisor. Regardless, you're not meeting the expectations of your role if you are withholding feedback from someone which could impact their life.

Perhaps I am the first person to ever tell you this, but someone had to give you the feedback so you have the opportunity to improve. As Maya Angelou once said, "Once you know better, do better." I believe that improving your ability to lean into the discomfort of delivering feedback will change your life and the lives of those you support, lead, love, or encounter. You may be thinking, "I know I should do it, but it's so uncomfortable and I don't want to make things awkward." I hear you. You're right, it's uncomfortable and it can be awkward, but it can become really uncomfortable and awkward when someone finds out that you've been holding out on giving them feedback for months, years, or even decades because you were uncomfortable.

If you really want to give the gift of feedback, you can use the **G.I.F.T. Framework** to help you navigate the best way to do so.

G.I.F.T. Framework—Give, Intend, Focus, Timely

G: Give Feedback

I know we've just discussed it, but it bears repeating. Are there circumstances in which you would decide not to give feedback when you know it is warranted? If so, don't worry, you're not alone. Many people avoid giving feedback because they may feel as though there is a lot going on in the world right now and there's no need to cause additional stress. It is important to use your Emotional Intelligence to assess the appropriate time and delivery but be sure that you are not projecting your fears or inability to handle feedback on others. Many people avoid giving feedback because they are unsure about how the recipient will react or just because the overall stress of delivering it at all. If you recall the statistic shared earlier in this book, 21% of people surveyed admitted that they avoid giving negative feedback (Harvard Business Review, 2017). Remember, in order for people to grow, they need you to be courageous and give the feedback anyhow. Develop your skills and confidence so that you don't become a feedback hoarder. Their development depends on it!

When you give the feedback, be sure to give it directly to the person for which it was intended. You're probably wondering, what's the alternative? Well, some have opted to give "general feedback" to everyone instead of giving feedback directly to the person, hoping that the person who it was intended for actually picks up on your subtleties and changes their behavior. But this is not an effective delivery method. Giving general feedback is impersonal and can send others spinning out and struggling to process whether or not the feedback was intended for them, creating bigger problems for you to sort through. In order to make it meaningful and effective, you have to ensure that you have time set aside to look the person in the eye and give them the feedback directly. This will give you an opportunity to create a space of safety, trust, and acceptance.

I: Intention Check

Feedback is an inside job. You have to check your intentions before you deliver feedback to anyone. Your intentions impact your outcome. At the end of the day, your heart has to be in it. You have to want to truly help the person that you are providing the feedback to. If you do not care, neither will they. Your intention and motives are on full display in the conversation. Your motive can be detected by what you choose to give feedback on, the words you choose to use, and the tone in which it is delivered. Those observable items are influenced by the invisible things such as your thoughts, feelings, and goals. Your words are a reflection of what's in your heart. Doing an intention check before delivering feedback can bring you a great deal of clarity and help you reframe your delivery so that your intention and impact of the feedback are as closely aligned as possible.

Intention Check: Ask yourself the following questions before you deliver feedback:

1. Check Your Mind—Understanding your context

    c. What is the feedback?

    d. Why is this important to share?

    e. What are the facts?

2. Check Your Heart—Understanding your feelings

    a. How do you feel?

    b. Is it about you or them?

    c. What do you want for them?

    d. Your motives and feelings impact your delivery

3. Check Your Mouth—Understanding your speech

    a. What will you say?

    b. Words have power

    c. Be genuine and authentic

    d. "Your words are a reflection of what's in your heart"

4. Check your Eyes—Understanding your narrative

    a. What do you see when you look at this person?

    b. What are your blind spots?

    c. How might your blind spot influence the feed back experience?

F: Focused Feedback (B.E.S.T.)

When you provide feedback, it should be focused on one to two areas. If you have too much feedback to share, you might run the risk of the person experiencing feedback fatigue, the act of becoming mentally and emotionally overwhelmed by the opportunities to improve. Trying to improve in multiple areas at a time might feel impossible or like an arduous task. Focus the feedback on the B.E.S.T. things: Behavior, Effects, Solution, and Testing to get the most out of your feedback conversation.

Behavior: When giving constructive feedback, it is important to describe the specific behavior that you are trying to address. According to Officevibe, 17% of employees feel that the feedback they get is not specific. You should not deliver feedback until you are clear about the gap between the current behavior and the desired behavior. Without clarity, they will not be able to fully address or improve their behavior. Be clear about the gap between the desired behavior and their actual performance. This will set the context for the conversation.

Effect: It is important for the recipient to have a clear understanding of why this is such a critical behavior to address. The behavior can have an effect on the recipient, the goals, the team, the family, the project, the assignment, or the organization. If they understand the negative effects of their behavior, they are more likely to change. Provide specific examples of the effects to solidify their understanding of why the behavior needs to be redirected.

Solution: It is important that you avoid admiring the problem and focus on solutions. This is a great opportunity for you to work together as thought partners to find the right solution for the recipient. This should be a brainstorm and not a directive. Allow the recipient to vocalize their thoughts on the support, resources, or training that they need in order to get back on track. Ask them how you can help support their next steps. It is also important that you thank the recipient for problem-solving and being committed to their own development. Saying thank you can go a long way.

Testing: When giving feedback, it is also important to have a discussion about where the recipient might be able to test or try out the solutions they decide to pursue to address the feedback. Getting them to reflect on when and where they might be able to test out their ideas and build their skills can prove to be very helpful when driving behavior change. This might assist the recipient with building in the motivation to apply feedback by having practical places where they can measure their progress.

Your feedback should be tailored to the recipient. The feedback should include specific examples that allow them to see their area of opportunity. When feedback is general or lacks specificity, it does not carry any meaning to the recipient. When you personalize it, it shows that you care. You care enough to know the details and care enough to speak with them about how to improve.

T: Timely Feedback

Timing is of the essence when it comes to feedback. The closer the feedback to the behavior that is triggering the feedback, the better! This gives the individuals the ability to recall behaviors described. Waiting to deliver feedback until the report card or the performance review is much too late to give feedback. You want to be sure that people have the opportunity to make changes to their behaviors before milestone evaluations are in the picture.

The Gift of Feedback in Motion

As a Talent Development professional, I have always been a part of the new hire experience, welcoming new employees to almost every organization that I've had the honor of being a part of. I truly enjoy being a part of the employee onboarding experience, you get to meet so many new people…people who will be driving the daily operations of the business, creating strategy for future opportunities, future leaders of the organization, and people who will help co-create an amazing culture that we all get to enjoy and love. Truth be told, I have a soft spot for new hires. Starting a new job, changing careers, making new friends, learning new skills, and reporting to a new boss can make almost anybody nervous. Everyone I meet is typically eager to fit in, to feel as though they belong and want to feel a sense of security in their decision to join the organization. They typically want to prove to themselves that they have what it takes to do the job and that they will be able to have a lasting career within the organization. I made it my personal mission to ensure that all new hires felt comfortable, welcomed, seen, and appreciated. I focused on providing them with the support and training they needed to flourish so that they could achieve their personal and professional goals.

If you truly want to see the power of feedback, just join any well-developed new hire training class. The onboarding training process can sometimes feel intimidating, especially if their training performance is tied to their ability to continue with the company. People are craving feedback as they are desperate to learn and are motivated and eager to do well. As a leader, it was my job to provide feedback during the onboarding process so that each employee had an equal opportunity to accelerate their growth over the course of the training. They had a safe space to practice their newly learned skills or work through how to transfer their existing skills to their new role.

My role in the training classes was quite involved and I took it very seriously. I kept a log of everyone's performance (test scores, behavioral assessments, classroom behaviors, role plays) and had one-on-one conversations with every trainee. If someone did something well, I gave them reinforcing feedback. If there was an opportunity to improve or make a slight tweak to their performance, I gave them developmental feedback. They would also get feedback from their peers as well as other leaders and employees throughout the training. To me, the formula was simple: it was our organizational duty to get them as much information as possible about the desired behaviors and how their daily performance tracked to that goal. It was our job to set each trainee up for success. In a few short weeks of training and feedback, I have seen countless new hires come in with very little knowledge, feeling uneasy about their abilities, emerge confident, excited, and fully capable of carrying out the core functions of their jobs. I credit it all to feedback.

In each new-hire training class, I prepared the employees for the feedback-rich learning environment we had cultivated. We tried to normalize feedback as a part of the developmental process, but no matter what I said, you could tell people were apprehensive and perhaps skeptical about feedback being called developmental. I could tell that many of the trainees had feedback baggage. Feedback baggage *refers to past negative experiences or ideas related to feedback that might weigh a person down and keep them from being open to feedback.* And like baggage, all of the details are tucked away for no one to see, but when you lift it up, you can feel just how heavy it is. I think carrying baggage from one experience to the next is common, but definitely detrimental to fully experiencing the power of feedback. If you believe that feedback is only given when you are about to lose a job, a friendship, or an opportunity, that's a heavy piece of baggage to carry.

During one of my new-hire training classes, I had a trainee who was in need of some feedback. He was outgoing, fully engaged, and participated in every discussion, role play, and activity we had with the group. We were in our third day of training when I realized a pattern: he seemed to talk over everyone in the room, and when presented with an opposing view, he would become defensive and would shut down physically and emotionally. In the spirit of giving feedback, I had a chat with him during the break and tried to understand more about his experience and share my observations with him. What I thought was a great conversation turned into tears. He began to make connections between the feedback I had given him and the feedback he believe he had never received at his previous job. He stated, "Thank you for sharing this with me. Is this why I wasn't able to move up at my previous job? I worked there for all of those years and could never move up." He thanked me for having the courage to tell him, wiped his tears, and then went back to class. He had been waiting for this feedback for years, and you could tell that he was grateful. He had a look that said, "I am finally in a position to do something about it." Feedback is truly a gift, no matter how difficult it might be to hear.

Questions are a powerful way to plant a seed and get people thinking about potential behaviors they might not be exhibiting today. One of the most memorable pieces of feedback I received was delivered in the form of a question: "Have you ever thought about going to college?" This was important feedback, because up until that point, no one in my family had been to college, so I had never really thought about it. But the question sparked my interest and made me ask myself more questions, causing me to see potential that I never saw before. I thought, "Could I go to college?" and "What did she see that tells her I could?" When I shared that I didn't think that I could afford it, she also went on to tell me how my athletic ability could be a means to achieving that goal. I thought, "Did I really have the athletic potential to earn a scholarship?" In the end, that feedback sparked a new thought and potential direction in my life. I began to believe that college was a possibility and that belief inspired a work ethic and discipline that I executed each day following. Maybe I could go to college? The sheer thought that it was a possibility fueled a fire that could not be squelched. I eventually earned an athletic scholarship and became the first in my family to go to college. Once I accomplished that goal, my thoughts about my potential to achieve more grew as I eventually pursued my Master's Degree and Doctoral Degree. Who would have thought that a question could spark that much self-inquiry? The feedback I received in high school from Triss Carter, Cross-Country Coach for Ygnacio Valley High School, was a gift that changed my life.

I am confident that my story is not unique. I am sure that if you were to look over the course of your life, you, too, would find examples of how feedback has helped to inform your choices and shape the person you have become at this very moment. Believe it or not, there was a piece of feedback you picked up somewhere that encouraged you to even look into this very book. What are the pivotal feedback moments in your life? How have they shaped the person you have become? Bringing these stories to the forefront of your conscious mind can help you remember how much you value and need feedback. Reflecting on these stories from time to time will keep you in a space of gratitude and can ease any hesitation you have about the feedback process.

Using Buffer Statements

Have you ever heard the phrase, "Don't take this personally" before receiving feedback? People use it because they simply struggle with just opening the conversation, so many people use it as a buffer to soften the perceived blow they believe people would feel from constructive feedback. Is it your *intention* to deliver a blow to their ego? Were you planning on hurting their feelings? If not, why attempt to package it in a way that softens it? The fact that we attempt to soften it sends the signal to the receiver that this is going to hurt...so it does!

Have you ever done this? Have you tried to prepare someone for your feedback? While the statement seems to be for the benefit of the receiver, I actually believe it's really designed to help the sender. There's another variation of this statement that many use as a buffer. Have you ever heard someone start off a conversation with, "I don't want you to take this personally but..."? If you have heard this phrase, then someone was getting ready to give you some feedback! And that leading statement suggests that it was not going to be nice.

The "I don't want you to take this personally" phrase usually has a follow-up statement that could pack a powerful punch and leave you reeling for days, even weeks! Let's be honest, I have had some feedback given to me that I still remember and it was from ten years ago! But is it really the follow-up statement that causes the most pain? Or is it the leading statement that sets the tone for how the feedback will be interpreted?

My guess is that you would say that it's the follow-up statement that causes the most pain. This is where they tell you what you've done wrong, where you have fallen short, and failed to demonstrate desired behavior or results. That's always painful to hear. I do not think there are many people who wake up and say, "I want to miss my goals today" or "I want to do everything wrong today." We all intend to show up as the best version of ourselves and we set out to do well. At least most people do, right?

I want to challenge your thoughts on this subject. What if I told you that it's not the follow-up statement that causes the most pain but the leading statement that begins the shift? When you tell someone, "I don't want you to take this personally," you automatically set the conversation up to have a negative tone. You may be thinking, how? Well, when you tell someone not to take it personally, you're really telling them not to get upset about what you are about to say…because it is going to upset them. So, in essence, you have already gotten them upset before you even told them your point. If that is the case, do you really think they are in a position to hear your "life-changing feedback"? If they are already on the defense due to your leading statement, do you think they are going to want to implement whatever you have to say next? No, not at all.

I thought it might be interesting to put this theory to the test, so I polled a few people in my network to gauge their initial thoughts when they heard the phrase, "I don't want you to take this personally but…" Here are the results:

Table 1

Gut Responses to the statement: "Don't take this personally but"

Theme	Rank	Count by Individual (N=67)
Negative Reaction	1	(73%)
Neutral Reaction	2	(22%)
Positive Reaction	3	(4%)

Note: N = 67

Only 4% of people indicated that they have positive thoughts about that phrase. Some people said, "I approach it with curiosity rather than judgement" or "It could be said out of love and wanting you to remember you might get defensive." There were 22% of people who indicated that the relationship would influence whether or not they interpreted that statement positively or negatively. Seventy-three percent expressed that the phrase created a negative feeling for them. Some people stated, "I get defensive immediately" or "my guard automatically goes up" or "I immediately brace myself" and "I instantly take it personally." I think these results speak to the true impact of this phrase. People do not want you to tell them not to take it personally! I don't know about you, but if I am preparing to give someone feedback and they are thinking any one of those thoughts above, chances are that my follow-up statement is going to be like adding fuel to a fire!

It is important that we think intentionally about delivering feedback, especially when it comes to the workplace. According to a Gallup Survey (2018), 79.6% of people surveyed were either passively or actively looking for a job after receiving negative feedback. In addition, 89% of employees reported being actively disengaged after receiving negative feedback. This does not mean for us to avoid giving negative feedback, but it certainly creates more urgency for us to develop our skills around being as effective as possible when delivering constructive feedback. It is my hope that this chapter helped you to think intentionally about practical ways you might enhance the delivery of your feedback so that you can make it the gift that keeps on giving.

Delivering Positive Feedback

Positive feedback is such an important part of our growth, development, and overall well-being. It is a form of recognition that helps people feel seen, valued, and appreciated. Many believe that giving positive feedback is an easy thing to do. Just say "good job" or "well done" and that should suffice. Or better yet, give them an enthusiastic high-five or thumbs-up with no words at all and that should really do the trick. It's not really that simple. When delivering positive feedback, make sure you are specific about the behavior you're praising and why it deserves recognition. When you add this level of specificity, it makes the feedback more meaningful and increases the likelihood that the behavior will be repeated.

Positive feedback can also come in the form of encouragement or a nudge. When you encourage people to try new things, like apply for a new job or volunteer for a project, you signal to them that you believe they have the potential to do well. Your belief in their ability might give them the confidence they need to step out of their comfort zone and try something new, creating new possibilities and outcomes that may never have existed if you did not nudge them to do so.

Encouragement is positive feedback about your potential. I have experienced the impact of encouragement first-hand. It was my freshman year at Ygnacio Valley High School and like every other freshman, I was nervous, uncertain, and needed reassurance in myself and my abilities. I joined the track team and felt right at home when I stepped onto the track. It was a team atmosphere and the coaches were supportive and patient with everyone as we all were trying to figure out our talents. I competed in the 4 × 100 relay, 100-meter dash, as well as the 200-meter dash. During our track meet at College Park High School, my coach, Robert Poulos, approached me about trying out a new event, the long jump. I was shocked and honestly hesitant about giving it a try. This was an actual meet and I had never even attempted the long jump before. I told him I didn't know what to do and he said it was easy—"just run and jump." My heart was racing and my mind was pacing, wanting to immediately decline because this was an actual meet; I didn't want to embarrass myself. The look in his eyes quickly calmed my nerves. He looked at me with a confidence and belief that inspired me to give it a shot. I competed in the long jump that day. I don't remember how I fared among the group, but I remember feeling excited and inspired about learning this new craft. Little did I know that four years later, it would not only become my favorite event and passion, but it would draw college recruitment offers that became my ticket to college and a whole new life! Coach Poulos, your nudge, encouragement, and positive feedback, changed my life. I will forever be grateful. Thank you for the nudge.

Reflection Questions

1. What resonated with you the most in this chapter?

2. Are there times that you've withheld the gift of feedback? Why?

3. How do you think people feel when they leave your presence after you deliver feedback?

4. What's one thing you can do to improve your ability to deliver feedback?

5. Is there someone you can encourage or nudge?

CHAPTER SIX

Receiving Feedback

"When you seek feedback with a motive that is focused on feeding your development versus feeding your ego, then and only then will you find the true value of feedback."—Dr. Shanita Williams

Have you ever been so excited to receive a gift, only to open it and find out that it was not at all what you expected? Those gifts that make you wonder, what did I say or do that made them send this exercise equipment my way? It's not about being ungrateful, it's just the cognitive dissonance one experiences when you are not expecting something. We've all been there and the experience is not so different when it comes to feedback.

Let's be honest, feedback is truly the gift that you love to hate. You love feedback because it gives insight into how you're doing, what's working well, and where you can tweak things a bit. On the other hand, people struggle with feedback because sometimes the way that it's delivered can make you either want to run and hide or pull out your verbal judo to defend yourself! It's challenging because you have no control over who gives it to you, how they give it to you and where they give it to you. And even when feedback is delivered perfectly and packaged beautifully, sometimes hearing it just hurts, leaving you wishing that they never told you at all! But the truth of the matter is, feedback is really a gift, even if it is one that is unexpected. When you have this additional insight, it provides you with the opportunity to transform, self-correct, and position yourself for a better performance, better relationship, and more importantly, a better future. This insight is invaluable and can be one of the greatest gifts you have ever received if you have the right mentality.

Feedback is an inside job. You have to be in strong mental and emotional shape in order to handle constructive criticism. You have to be able to regulate the information coming in, control the emotions that emerge as a result, and manage your response to the sender in the moment. If your feedback muscles are weak, you will lack the mental and emotional stamina and strength that is needed to endure a difficult conversation which could end up hurting your ego, your relationships, and in some cases, your career.

In the previous chapter, we uncovered two behaviors that can make you vulnerable when receiving feedback: Labeling and Leaning Out. Labeling is the process of attributing negative characteristics to the individual delivering the feedback in effort to dismiss or minimize the value of the feedback. Leaning out is the display of body posture that sends a signal that you might be either disinterested or in disagreement with the feedback being delivered. Body language is a powerful communication tool and accounts for the majority of the messages that people use to interpret a situation. Leaning out can be as subtle as shifting your weigh to the back of your chair, or as obvious as leaning back so far in your chair you might just fall out. I am not a behavioral psychologist, but it makes sense that if you heard something that you disagreed with or was near something that you thought would hurt you, you'd naturally back away from the sender.

I remember giving someone constructive feedback one day. She was upset that she was in the office on a day that she preferred to be home due to weather conditions. She walked around the office slamming drawers and huffing so loudly that it disrupted those in the office, so I asked her over to understand what was going on. She proceeded to give me feedback: she leaned in and pulled out a copy of an email I had sent about the work from home options where she circled, underlined, and highlighted the area she wanted to discuss. I did not expect this to happen but I leaned in anyway as I was genuinely curious as to why she was upset. I asked questions and was intent on hearing her perspective. Shortly after, I proceeded to give her feedback about her behavior (there was a trend already brewing) and she immediately leaned out. I mean, she leaned so far back that she was almost out of my office. She crossed her arms to further signal that she was not interested, not in agreement, and I soon realized that she was not listening to a word I was saying.

To improve your ability to receive feedback, you have to condition your mind so that you have the strength to navigate those feedback conversations. Thoughts have the power to influence your behavior and outcome. Use the following framework to remain open to feedback by shaping your thoughts so that you can learn and lean in versus label and lean out.

O.P.E.N. Framework: Observe, Probe, Express Thanks, Next Steps

Observe: Receiving negative feedback can trigger a great deal of emotion and those emotions impact the way we think and the way be behave. You have to be able to observe both your thoughts (labeling vs. learning) and body language (leaning out vs. leaning in) in real time so that you can get the most out of the feedback experience. Take 100% responsibility for your emotional experience (Kofman, 2006). You have to be very self-aware to notice what emotions you are feeling and where the source of that emotion lies. Many believe, "they made me mad" or "they make me this way." It's important to understand that your thoughts about what they said are really the source of the pain and thus the reasons for your emotional experience. Observe and examine that, and you'll be able to take full ownership of your emotional experience and begin to control it. If you want to refocus your brain on learning and leaning in, here's how:

Muscle Building Skills

1. Take notes. Writing down their feedback will help you focus on what is being said instead of judging what is being said.

2. Consciously shift your body forward toward your note book in front of you to remain engaged.

Probe: The brain is wired to fight, flee, or freeze during times of stress or when it senses danger. Many times, people sit passively when receiving feedback, quickly jump to defending themselves when receiving feedback, or avoid the feedback altogether by avoiding the person, the call, the meeting, or the email. Let's be honest, all feedback given to you is not always clearly communicated or delivered. There's an African Proverb that says, "Examine what is said and not who speaks." It is important that you do not get caught up in who is delivering the feedback and how the person is delivering the feedback, but truly try to understand the essence of their message. You cannot understand it if you engage in a debate.

A healthy way to respond is to approach it from a place of curiosity. Ask clarifying questions so that you can understand their perspective and leverage the information they are trying to convey. Remember, ontological humility is all about understanding that there is more than one perspective of the truth. Asking questions to better understand their truth of the situation will put you in a better position to respond. But start with asking questions first; resist the urge to defend, deflect, or derail. Questions are the key to dialogue and are the hallmark of a healthy feedback mentality.

Muscle Building Questions

1. Can you give me a specific example of what you observed so that I can better understand your perspective?
2. Can you tell me more about that?
3. What does success look like for this behavior?
4. What recommendations or suggestions do you have for the future?

Express: Once you've spent time understanding their perspective and purpose of the feedback, it's important that you take the time to express two things: your understanding and thanks. Playing back your understanding of the feedback is an important part of the feedback process. Ensuring that you've fully heard and understood the information that was shared helps you ensure that you have accurately captured their sentiments and sets you up to address next steps that will help impact the area discussed, should you decide to take action. In the book, Conscious Business, author Kofman stated, "You must take unconditional responsibility; you need to see yourself as a 'player,' as a central character who has contributed to shape the current situation – and who can thus affect its future." Think about your role in this feedback and what you can take responsibility for, and be sure to express it. This activates a sense of ownership and agency to impact the future.

In addition, it is important to express gratitude and appreciation for their willingness to share the feedback with you. Remember, some people choose to withhold feedback. Let them know how much you appreciate their candor and courage. It will reinforce that you have a growth-mindset and willingness to learn, which will increase the likelihood that they will give you feedback in the future. In addition, it fosters psychological safety and trust. If people feel safe to bring feedback to your attention without damaging the relationship, they will do it again.

Muscle Building Questions

1. What is my understanding of the feedback?
2. What can I take responsibility for? How can I use that information to impact the future?
3. What do I appreciate about this feedback?

Next steps: Once you have completed the conversation, you've finished the hard part and can breathe. Now you have to think about your next steps and what you will do with the feedback you received. Many leave feedback conversations feeling as though they know what to do and run out of the room creating plans without fully thinking things through. Others leave the feedback conversation feeling as though they can put a plan together, but when they are alone, they find themselves stuck, maybe even swirling a bit. The next two chapters will give you guidance for making your next steps meaningful and intentional as we discuss Processing Feedback, the mental act of analyzing the internal narrative attached to feedback, and Applying Feedback, the process of prioritizing and acting on feedback.

Muscle Building Skills

1. Synthesize notes and ideas so that you do not forget the details of the discussion.
2. Take a moment to pause and reflect prior to acting on the feedback.

Continuing Feedback Muscle Development

"We can't just sit back and wait for feedback to be offered, particularly when we're in a leadership role. If we want feedback to take root in the culture, we need to explicitly ask for it."—Ed Batista

O.P.E.N. Framework will help you stay present while you are receiving feedback in the moment. But do you want to wait until you are in a feedback conversation before you build your feedback muscles? If you'd like to continue developing your ability to receive feedback, here are some practical tips you can do today to start building your feedback resilience:

1. Solicit Feedback—There are 365 days in a year. If you challenge yourself to ask one person a week (what can you do to improve), you will wire your brain to not only handle constructive feedback, but anticipate constructive feedback.

Here are some questions that help garner feedback:

    a. "What's one thing I can do to improve [x]?"

    b. "If we could make this process better, what would you suggest?"

    c. "What are some areas that you feel could use some refinement?"

    d. "How would you approach that same scenario?"

2. Solicit Positive Feedback Daily—Soliciting feedback is not always about identifying your deficits, it's also about identifying your strengths so that you can leverage them as well. Soliciting positive feedback also helps to build a healthy emotional and mental response to feedback in that it trains the brain to not always activate the "amygdala highjack" because it perceives feedback to be something that you have to defend yourself against. By training your mind to also see and hear the positives that are connected to feedback, you can truly start to see feedback as a gift and create a healthy approach to feedback.

Here are some questions you can ask to solicit positive feedback:

    a. "What did you like about [x]?"

    b. "What did I do well?"

    c. "What would you say my strengths are?"

3. Give Yourself Feedback—You know yourself better than anyone! Take some time to play back your day and identify small things you can do to make the next day better. We are usually our worst critic. If you can handle feedback from yourself, you can handle feedback from anyone! You just have to make the time to slow down and write out some actionable steps. Don't forget to balance your feedback with positives as well; those may be harder to catch but just as important to our overall development. You can use our feedback journal to keep track of your progress.

Receiving Positive Feedback

Believe it or not, receiving positive feedback can be an uncomfortable experience for many. I have seen countless people literally squirm in their seats when I told them about how great they were or how much I appreciated their efforts. It's a really interesting phenomenon to witness. Why is it so difficult to hear about your accomplishments, successes, or strengths? Many even go so far to reject positive feedback and transition into a conversation about what they did wrong and highlight their shortcomings? Why is it so much easier to talk about our mistakes than our successes? I believe that we have been conditioned as a society to always look for what's wrong versus what's right. We honestly do not have a lot of practice with hearing positive feedback because every conversation seems to hover around our opportunities. When receiving positive feedback, no need to say anything other than, "thank you" or "thank you very much" or "I appreciate that thank you." Fully embrace the positivity and take it all in. You deserve it.

Receiving feedback is truly an art and takes tremendous emotional intelligence to navigate with grace and humility. Remember to focus on what is being said, not the sender themself so that you are able to hear the feedback in its entirety. Feedback has the power to unlock or limit your potential, both of which can change the trajectory of your life. It's important to note that the power does not come from the feedback alone; the real power lies in what you decide to do or not do with the feedback. Remember, feedback is information about the past or present that has the potential to influence the future. You must never forget that you have the power of choice when it comes to feedback and as such, your choices influence your outcomes. You are not required to do anything with it. Feedback simply empowers you to make informed decisions about your future…and that is the real essence of power.

Questions to ponder:

1. Do I lean in or lean out during my feedback conversations?

2. When were the times that I labeled feedback as negative? If I were to remove the label, is there something that I might learn?

3. How comfortable am I with expressing my understanding of the feedback that was shared?

4. What positive feedback should I hold onto?

CHAPTER SEVEN

Processing Feedback

"Be careful what you say about yourself, because you are listening."
—Lisa M. Hayes

We've discussed the challenges with delivering feedback and receiving feedback, but there is an area of feedback we have not yet tackled and one that is rarely discussed: the art of processing feedback. While receiving feedback is all about how to remain calm, cool, and collected in the face of feedback, processing feedback is about what happens after it is delivered, the sender leaves, and you're sitting there alone with just your thoughts and theirs. Receiving feedback is what they say to you; processing feedback is what you say to yourself. What do you do with the gift they so kindly left in your lap?

One day, I was in a meeting with a few colleagues discussing an exciting change that was going to impact the organization. It was going to be a huge change and required all hands on deck. We came to the point in the meeting where it was decision time and we needed to discuss next steps. The leader of the meeting posed a timeline that I thought was much too aggressive, but I didn't say anything aloud. All of a sudden, a voice emerged in all of the silence and said, "Based on Shanita's face, I don't think she agrees with the timeline." I was shocked. Did that just happen? Yeah, it did—in front of the entire group. I immediately told myself to fix my face so I immediately plastered a joker-like smile on my face. I am not sure that it helped my cause at all. I had so many things running through my mind. Why would they said this aloud, let alone in front of everyone? What was their motive? I wanted to yell out, "hey guy, this is just my face," but part of me wanted to run out of the room. I was embarrassed. Some of the people in the meeting were individuals that I was meeting for the first time, so I was worried about what they would think of me. His comment sparked a flurry of thoughts that I was left to process: "They think I am not onboard, they think I am not a team player, they think I am negative." Have you ever had anyone comment on your face? Getting feedback on your facial expressions is not new for many. I know several people who now feel like they have to smile as big as a cheerleader, just to avoid having someone ask if they are upset, if they are okay, or if something is wrong. Yes, people can give you feedback about anything, including your face. It's how you process the feedback that counts.

Processing feedback can be quite complex. Feedback can send you into a downward spiral, questioning your very existence, self-esteem, self-image, and overall self-worth…ruminating for hours, days, months, or even years! As your responsibilities grow, your network expands, and your influence increases, so does the amount of feedback you receive as well. And what do you do when you have a stack of these beautiful gifts of feedback from various sources? If unprepared, many people find themselves soaking up all of the feedback they receive only to feel frustrated, overwhelmed, or over-analyzing their every move to the point of paralysis. Instead of soaking up every single drop of information and holding onto it all, we will teach you how to process the feedback, holding onto the most significant themes and lessons that would have the greatest impact. We will discuss how to drop the Sponge Mentality and adopt the Strainer Mentality.

It was a typical day at work. I had a few one-on-one sessions with my team, a one-on-one with my leader, a project meeting with a work stream, and facilitating a training for a large group. It was the start of a very busy but productive day. I had finally grabbed some lunch and made my way back to my desk to prepare for my all-hands meeting for my department. That day stands out in my mind because it was the day I had received a great deal of feedback, both directly and indirectly. Between the training surveys, employee engagement surveys, the feedback from my supervisor, feedback from my employees, the live feedback I received from my trainees…and all of the feedback I had been carrying from the day before, the week before, the month before, ten years before suddenly came crashing down on me at this one moment. I felt the weight of the feedback wash all over me. It felt like I was underwater, I could feel myself getting panicked… My mind was replaying the feedback and trying to implement it into my upcoming meeting but I couldn't think clearly. I noticed my inner critic pop up as I started to label myself as "unworthy," an "imposter" telling myself that my feelings were signs that I was not fit to be in the role. I knew that my feelings and thoughts were not productive and I had a meeting that was set to happen in a few minutes.

I needed some fresh air. I went for a walk and asked a co-worker to join me. I had never asked him to go for a walk… I am sure my face looked like I was in need of help. He kindly obliged and followed me down the hall. I was on the brink of tears and I didn't know why. We finally stopped and he asked me what was going on and I said, "I don't think I am good enough to do this job." I went on a rant about all of the feedback I received as though it was evidence that I was right. I don't remember his exact words to me, but I remember him telling me to take a breath and reassuring me that I was in the position for a reason. How did I get to this point? The "body expresses what the mind represses" (Hoffman Institute, 2020). Something was clearly happening internally.

If you haven't picked this up already, feedback is an inside job. You can have tons of information presented to you from the external environment but it's not at all useful until you examine what's going on in your internal environment—your internal response and narrative attached to the processing of the information. Looking inside oneself is an uncomfortable and messy process, but it's one of the most important things you can do. You have to be willing to do the hard work. That is, be willing to look inside your heart and inside your mind to examine the feelings and narratives attached to the feedback you've received. Because you have feelings, thoughts, and narratives attached to the feedback you receive, they can influence your behavior and ultimately influence how you see yourself, your worth, your value, your ability, and your future.

Sponge and Strainer Mentality

There are two ways to process feedback, with a Sponge Mentality or Strainer Mentality. The Sponge Mentality is the unconscious process of holding onto all feedback you encounter, regardless of their value. Having a Sponge Mentality can put you at risk of becoming overwhelmed. When presented with feedback, we tend to take it all in, hold onto it for an indefinite amount of time, replaying and ruminating on the feedback and filling in the gaps with our own counterproductive stories and feelings about what they shared. Remember, some feedback is destructive; holding onto destructive feedback is unhealthy and can impact your over-all self-esteem.

When you have a Sponge Mentality and hoard feedback indefinitely, it is possible to suffer from feedback fatigue, the act of becoming mentally and emotionally tired from constantly scanning your environment and finding opportunities to improve. If you feel oversaturated with feedback, you might miss out on meaningful feedback simply because you do not have the space or capacity to take on more. The goal is to adopt a healthier way to process feedback: the Strainer Mentality. Tim Fargo once said, "Mistakes should be examined, learned from, and discarded; not dwelled upon and stored." The Strainer Mentality is the conscious process of examining feedback, holding onto the feedback that is meaningful, identifying learning, and releasing the feedback that no longer serves you.

Oprah said, "what you dwell on, you become." It's time to improve your ability to process feedback so that you can become what you want to become regardless of the feedback received. You have to condition your mind to respond appropriately, to take control of the narrative. The L.O.V.E Framework will help you drop the Sponge Mentality and adopt the Strainer Mentality.

L.O.V.E. Framework—Let Go, Override, Visualize, Examine

When it comes to processing feedback, it's all about L.O.V.E. and loving yourself first and foremost. It was RuPaul who said, "If you don't love yourself, how in the hell you gonna love somebody else?" We have to practice self-love and self-care by taking care of our mind and being thoughtful about what we let in. It is important that we take control of our thoughts and engage in metacognition, thinking about our thinking. We have to be more conscious of the subconscious thoughts and feelings that are guiding our behaviors each and every day. This framework will help you do the hard but necessary work to improve your ability to process feedback.

Let Go: Why do you think that the Frozen song, "Let It Go" was and is still so very popular? It's because we all have things that we hold onto that we know we need to let go. There's not an adult in the world who doesn't sing that song and think about all of the baggage we have held onto all of these years. In life, we accumulate experiences and emotions and unresolved issues that we've been holding onto throughout our lives. Bob Marley said, "Emancipate yourself from mental slavery." When we hold onto the pain of the past, it makes it difficult for us to be fully present which can inadvertently impact our future. You may have destructive feedback that you have held onto that you keep playing over and over in your mind. The Strainer Mentality gives you the opportunity to let destructive feedback come in and strain itself right out, because it does not get to stay. Do not give negative thoughts and emotions the ability to cement its claws into the recesses of your mind. Destructive feedback is like weeds—it's hard to contain and difficult to get rid of once it's there.

You may have heard, "sticks and stones may my break my bones but words will never hurt me." I cannot remember how many times I heard parents tell their children to say that growing up. In reality, the words did hurt. There are many people who carry the pain of destructive feedback with them for years. Yes, painful comments and words go home with people at night, may follow them into their dreams, and can stay with them for years.

When it comes to letting go and successfully processing feedback, it is important to understand what our triggers are. Triggers are the topics or areas in our life that are more sensitive to negative feedback. It's the areas of your life that make feedback feel very personal even if it is not meant to be. Understanding the things that trigger feelings of fear, inadequacy, incompetence, defensiveness, or inferiority can help you manage the mental tape that plays in your mind if feedback happens to activate a past trauma or experience. Triggers are unique to the individual so it's important that we spend time learning more about ourselves so that we can manage our response to them and let them go!

How do you let it go? Emotions are energy that move in and out of our bodies. To move the negative thoughts and emotions out so that we can let it go, engaging in exercises that helps your conscious mind understand that it can indeed let it go is helpful. Exercises like writing things down and shredding it or burning it can be helpful. Journaling your thoughts to get them "out" of your head and your heart can be such a powerful experience as well. Find the mindfulness technique that works for you, but you have to discharge the things that are no longer serving you so that you can make space for the things that are.

Muscle Building Skills:

1. Identify feedback baggage and feedback triggers.
2. Engage in a symbolic act that demonstrates to your conscious mind that you are letting it go and straining that feedback.

Once we become more conscious of the subconscious thoughts and feelings that are guiding our behaviors each and every day, we maintain our agency and ability to manage the outcomes we pursue. It is important to take inventory of the thoughts and feelings we collect over time and work diligently to clean out our mental closet so that nothing is preventing us from living and becoming the best versions of ourselves. You have so much potential and a purpose to fulfill in this world. You do not want to let a limiting belief limit your potential and overall impact on the world.

Override limiting beliefs: It has been said that the average human being has over 60,000 thoughts per day and the majority of them are negative and/or counterproductive. Most of our thoughts are not articulated aloud but running in the background subconsciously, directing our every move. Have you ever heard the words, "I can't do that" or "I'm not smart enough" or "I always make mistakes" or "I'm not good enough"? Those are examples of limiting beliefs, thoughts that limit your potential. Think about it—if you believe you're not smart enough to go to college, would you go through the effort of applying? If you think that you always make mistakes, would you be willing to put yourself out there and try something new? If you think you're not good enough to lead a team, would you apply for a leadership role even if you were encouraged? Willie Nelson said, "Once you replace negative thoughts with positive ones, you'll start having positive results." It's important that you take inventory of the limiting beliefs you have operating in the back of your mind and rewrite the narrative so that you have more opportunity to explore and expand your potential.

Sometimes limiting beliefs can be disguised as little humble statements that have no intention of harming you but they can certainly influence and shape your behaviors. One day, I was in a meeting with someone I had just met. I was impressed by his knowledge, wisdom, and years of experience and looked forward to learning from him. In our second meeting, I shared that I was excited to learn from him and that I was open to feedback along the way as it was my first time tackling a project of this nature. I also said that I was young in my leadership journey so I appreciated any coaching or support he could provide. He immediately asked me if he could offer me some coaching in that very moment. I agreed, but was unsure about what he'd coach me on since we've only met twice. He told me, "You are not young in your leadership journey, you have been leading all of your life and I am sure people have followed you." I paused and thought, *wow!* I didn't realize that I had been carrying this thought with me into every conversation that I entered. How was that thought serving me? Did it give me permission to ask questions? Did it make me feel free from any expectations people may have had? It really made me think. It made me think about how that thought made me small, less important than others, invalidating my own lived experience, knowledge, and skills. We have to take stock of our thinking because it informs how we go about living. I am thankful that he gave me that feedback so that I could reframe my thinking.

After leaving a feedback session, you want to take a moment to examine your thoughts and feelings associated with the feedback that they give you or that you give yourself. Sometimes we develop negative thoughts about ourselves based upon what someone has shared or we take on a negative statement and hold on tight to it, blurring the line between their opinion and fact. We have to do the work to ensure we properly process the feedback and narratives attached. Here are some tips to help you build your feedback muscle:

Muscle Building Skills:

1. Ask: What's the story you're telling yourself?

2. Replace: Identify a less stressful narrative that opens up the aperture of possibilities.

Visualize success: Bob Proctor once said, "if you can conceive it in your mind, you can hold it in your hands." Being able to visualize your success with the feedback area that has been identified is certainly part of getting better. Research has shown that people who imagine themselves performing a task, improve their performance in that task without physically doing anything (Ranganathan, Siemionow, Sahgal and Yue, 2016). Mental imagery and visualization are great ways to help you improve your mental strength. As a college athlete, we would participate in visualization activities where we imagined the perfect execution of our craft. I was on the track and field team and competed in the long jump. They had us imagine every detail, engaging all five of our senses. What was I wearing? What was the weather like? How did it feel? How many steps did I take down the runway? Imagining my penultimate step and launching off the board into the sandy pit. I had to visualize my body positioning in the air and ultimately what the successful outcome would be. When I practiced this technique, it built my confidence and muscle memory so that I could achieve the success I desired.

Holding a positive mental image of what success looks like for you can be just as powerful with feedback. Imagine delivering that flawless presentation, imagine rocking that interview panel, imagine networking with strangers, and imagine building stronger relationships. It all starts in the mind. Your mind has to know what you want to achieve, and trust me, it will work hard to get there. Don't spend your time worrying about what can go wrong. Focus your mind on what could go right…and you'll nail it!

Muhammad Ali was famously known for saying, "I am the greatest of all times." I think it is important to not only visualize success but affirm that success with positive affirmations. Tell yourself, "I am capable, I am worthy, I am smart." Let those powerful statements cement themselves into your psyche. Feel the positive emotions associated with those statements and allow them to guide your behavior. I know some people feel as though positive affirmations feel empty. I agree, they can feel that way sometimes. That's why it's important to find affirmations that hold truth for you. Perhaps saying "I'm detailed oriented" feels fake to say when you really believe you are not. But what if it was "When I slow down, I am able to attend to the details." If that feels truer and more authentic to your experience, roll with it. Visualize your success and declare the victory in your mind. Your body will have no choice but to follow.

Muscle Building Questions and Skills:

1. What is the outcome you want to achieve?

2. Take three to five minutes each day to imagine yourself achieving the outcome.

3. Craft authentic statements that affirm and motivate you mentally and emotionally.

Examine the Learning: It is important to mentally process what YOU have learned from your feedback session. Most of the time you are listening and taking notes. Now is your time to reflect and think about what you specifically took away from the session. This is not about examining what action to take; it's about examining the learning. You cannot have a clear path to action if you have not clearly identified what you've taken from the conversation. If you are processing feedback and only thinking about what to do, you are not processing feedback, you're focused on applying the feedback. When you find that mental space where you can capture what you've learned and how this learning benefits you today and how it will help you in the future, then you know you're successfully processing the feedback experience.

Finding the learning when your ego is triggered can prove to be difficult. It is important to reflect on the feedback during a time when you are not feeling negative emotions, or else you'll end up missing the learning altogether. Give yourself some space from the feedback so that you can review it with a more objective lens. If you find that it is difficult to process after a few days, you might find it valuable to find a friend or a coach to give you an unbiased perspective and guide you through the process.

Muscle Building Questions:

1. What can I learn from this feedback?

2. How will this feedback serve me in the future?

Developing the muscle to effectively process the feedback we receive from others and the feedback we give ourselves can be one of the most challenging parts of the feedback experience. I remember starting my new job as an Associate Admissions Counselor. My job was to speak with students and then schedule an appointment for them with an Admission Counselor to complete their admission paperwork. After thirty days on the job, I was offered a promotion to Admission Counselor position due to my performance. After thirty days in my new role, something changed. I could not seem to schedule appointments and the ones that I did schedule did not show up. I was a nervous wreck. I was just promoted. What was going to happen? As you can imagine, my supervisor, Jenny Johnston, called me into the office to discuss my performance. It felt like I was going to the principal's office. I had a million thoughts flying through my mind. Is she going to write me up? Demote me? Fire me? Yell at me? Is she regretting her decision to promote me? We went in her office and she closed the door. Jenny was always bubbly and carefree. Her energy was different this time.

What happened next shocked me. She leaned in with care and compassion and said, "Where is my Shanita?" She went on to say that I wasn't the optimistic person that she was used to and that she noticed that I have been hard on myself. She went on to say, "I want that Shanita back, the strong, determined, capable, and confident Shanita." It was clear that I was in my head. I was not processing my performance in a healthy way. The feedback I was giving myself was that I was going to get fired and I was disappointing my manager. Those thoughts were clearly impeding my ability to bounce back after a setback and limiting my abilities and my potential. I remember her grabbing my hands, giving me a pep talk, and telling me that she believed in me. No reprimand. No write-up. No ultimatums. It was pure feedback with compassion. Jenny was always great at that. Holding you accountable while pointing you in the right direction and making you feel like you could fly. That feedback immediately changed my performance. By the end of the month, I exceeded my goals and more importantly, I proved to myself that I could do anything if I were able to believe in myself. I had to get rid of the thoughts that were holding me back. I had to remind myself of my abilities. Once I let go of the mental baggage, I was able to hear Jenny's call to action and step into my full potential. That feedback changed my performance and my professional experience overall. The compassion she showed me gave me permission to be compassionate to myself and do the work I needed to do to grow. Jenny, thank you for helping me process your feedback in a healthy way!

We have to be willing to step into a vulnerable space and examine the thoughts and feelings that create the most stress and discomfort. If we are able to successfully identify the thoughts that are limiting our potential, then and only then will we become empowered to enact change. Once you've done this work, you are ready to move forward and come up with a plan to apply the feedback to your life.

Questions to ponder:

1. What do I need to let go?

2. What thoughts or feelings are no longer serving me well?

3. What do I want to achieve in my life? What does successful achievement look like?

4. What am I learning about myself and how I process feedback?

CHAPTER EIGHT

Applying Feedback

"If you reject feedback, you also reject the choice of acting in a way that may bring you abundant success." — John Mattone

It's important to note that power does not come from the feedback alone. The real power lies in what you decide to do or not do with the feedback. Remember, feedback is information that has the potential to the influence future performance outcomes. You must never forget that you have the power of choice when it comes to feedback, and as such, your choices influence your outcomes. You are not required to do anything with it. Feedback simply empowers you to make informed decisions about your future... and that it the real essence of power. Who wouldn't want to have agency and power over their future?

As you begin the journey of applying feedback, there are two areas where we need to focus our energy if we are to become more effective at applying feedback:

1. **Reacting to feedback:** Quickly implementing actions to address the feedback with very little thought

2. **Neglecting feedback:** Failure to do anything with the feedback you've been given

I once wrote a research paper and moved it forward for feedback. I decided to send it to five people for feedback so that I was sure that the paper was at its best. One person responded and provided a great deal of feedback. I recall going through all of the track changes and simply clicking "accept" repeatedly. Then, when the next person provided feedback, I did the same thing… clicking "accept changes" repeatedly. By the time I incorporated the feedback from the fifth and final person, the feedback that I had accepted conflicted with other reviews and my paper was almost unrecognizable. I was now missing the mark on the deliverable altogether. I had to pause for a moment and regroup to figure out how to get back on track. How did I make it to this point? I was reacting to all of the feedback that was provided versus responding to feedback.

Reacting to feedback can sometimes make people feel good in the moment because you usually have a plan in your head about what you are going to do, before the person is even finished with giving you the feedback. It's like a mental checklist running through your mind that you begin to check off as soon as you leave the sender's presence. Sometimes the reaction is so quick that it feels subconscious and automatic. Responding involves engaging the heart and head in an analysis of what the best action should be. Without stepping back and really assessing what you've heard, you might miss the learning about your learning. That is, looking at your feedback in aggregate can give you new insight about what to prioritize and what actions are best. In my opinion, feedback without action is simply noise. It may take a bit more effort, but taking the time to S.I.F.T. through your feedback so that you can respond and prioritize can set you up for success!

S.I.F.T. Framework—Source, Impact, Frequency, Trend

When it comes to applying feedback, you have to S.I.F.T. through all the information you have received and make a conscious choice about where to focus. This is usually the most challenging part, especially if you have received a lot of feedback during the same timeframe. For some, they get bogged down and even paralyzed when it comes time to figuring out what to work on first. The benefit of using the S.I.F.T. Framework is that it allows you a period of honest reflection and introspection that can help propel you into action.

The framework challenges you to think about who provided the feedback (source), who the feedback touches (impact), how often you've heard this feedback (frequency), and the intersection of this feedback with various parts of your life (trend). I have added a point system to the model to assist with identifying which pieces of feedback you should work on first and which ones you can deprioritize to avoid feedback fatigue and the desire to neglect feedback altogether. For each piece of feedback, you would review the four areas of the S.I.F.T. Framework to help inform your next steps.

Source: The first thing you want to do is think about the source. The source is the person who delivered the feedback and helps provide context and clarity about the behavior they observed. When receiving feedback, I mentioned that you want to focus on what's being said, not who is saying it. That creates space for you to fully hear the feedback and process it effectively. However, when it comes to the application of the feedback, I think it's important to consider your relationship to the source as one of the factors that can help you decide how to prioritize your actions. We all have a variety of people that we interact with on a daily, weekly, and monthly basis. While feedback from everyone can provide tremendous learning, it is important to note that when it comes to prioritizing what you work on first, feedback from a stranger holds a different weight than feedback from someone with whom you have a trusting relationship. I have assigned point values to each so that you can objectively calculate where you should focus after all four areas of the model are assessed.

When you think about the SOURCES of feedback, you can think of them on three levels:

1. Trusted contact: Someone who knows you very well (3pts)

2. Acquaintance: Someone you interact with occasionally (2pts)

3. Stranger: Someone who does not know you (1pt)

Impact: Next, understanding the impact of the feedback on yourself, others, the assignment, or project is another vital element when it comes to determining how you would like to respond to the feedback. The impact can vary based on what is uncovered in your feedback session. There's not an exact science to calculating the impact—it's truly based up on your gut feelings. Regardless of the value that you select, it is important to think through how this behavior affects the various people, places, or things in your life. The greater the level of impact of the behavior, the more urgency one typically feels to correct the behavior.

When you think about the IMPACT of feedback, you can think of them on three levels:

1. Large: Large impact on myself and others (3pts)

2. Medium: Moderate impact on myself and others (2pts)

3. Small: Minimal impact on myself and others (1pt)

Frequency: Next, you want to examine the frequency of the feedback. Feedback that has been mentioned frequently compared to rarely might also be helpful information to reflect on. If you receive feedback on a behavior more than once, the behavior is clearly visible which may correlate with an increased level of impact. The more often the behavior is displayed, the greater the risk of affecting others. This will also give insight into how difficult of a behavior change this might be. When it comes to frequency, you also want to think about what might be influencing the behavior identified. Could it be a lack of knowledge, lack of skill, or would it require a shift in mindset? These things might give insight into what behavior is occurring and what work might be required to influence the change you'd like to see.

When you think about the FREQUENCY of feedback, you can think of them on three levels:

1. Mentioned more than three times (3pts)
2. Mentioned twice (2pts)
3. First time (1pt)

Trend: The last and final consideration to help prioritize feedback is examining the trends. Sometimes we see patterns of feedback that show up in multiple aspects of our lives. Other times, the feedback may be isolated in only one area of our lives. Either way, it is important to explore whether or not this is a consistent theme in your life. By slowing down and thinking about where the feedback shows up (work, home, school, etc.), you can position yourself to better plan your approach. It will also help you see the potential impact of improving this behavior in multiple areas of your life. For example, I always have a typo in my emails. I also have them in text messages, reports, presentations, and even social media posts. If I were to improve my ability to proofread and pay attention to the details, that one behavior would have a positive impact on five areas of my life. When it comes to S.I.F.T.-ing through the plethora of feedback and trying to figure out where to start, examining the intersection of the trends within your life can help you find the best place to start.

When you think about the TREND of feedback, you can think of them on three levels:

1. Three or more areas of life – for example: work, home, school (3pts)

2. Two or more areas of life – for example: work and home (2pts)

3. One area of your life: for example: work only (1pt)

Below is a copy of the S.I.F.T. Model. Take a piece of feedback and see if you can calculate what you should do with your feedback.

S.I.F.T. Model

Source	Impact	Frequency	Trend
(1pt) Stranger	(1pt) Small	(1pt) Mentioned Once	(1pt) Only in one area of your life
(2pt) Acquaintance	(2pt) Medium	(2pt) Mentioned Twice	(2pt) Two areas of your life
(3pt) Trusted Contact	(3pts) Large	(3pt) Mentioned 3x or more	(3pt) 3 or more areas of your life

© 2017 Shanita Williams

Source + Impact + Frequency + Trend = _____

Results

If your score is:

10-12: Prioritize this feedback. Develop an action plan.

7-9: This item holds merit. Work on these after you focus on other high-priority items.

6 or below: These items should be delayed or revaluated before creating an action plan.

Moving Feedback into Action

Now that you have prioritized your feedback and know where you'd like to start, it's time to begin developing a plan to address the specific areas identified. You can use our A.C.T. principles to help you with the development of your plan. **A.C.T.** stands for Assess, Create, Tell. These simple principles will help you think through key items to consider so that you can ensure successful implementation of the feedback:

Assess, Create, Tell

Assess: What do you need?

It is important that you take stock of what you need before prematurely moving into implementation. I have seen many receive feedback on what they should do differently but lack the skills or resources to carry it out. Even the most enthusiastic and well-intentioned individual will fail if they do not have what they need to implement the feedback. Ask yourself: Are there critical resources you need? Where can you get them? When will you get it? What are the barriers to getting what you need? Who can help you address those barriers? These questions are a good starting place to stimulate the internal inquiry needed to ensure your readiness for implementation.

Create: Create a Plan

It has been said, a goal without a plan is just a wish. It is critical to outline the steps you will take toward implementing the feedback, or you can find yourself wishing things were better and not actually working toward development. So, what is your plan? What are your milestones and indicators that you're on the right track? When will you start? What does success look like?

Tell: Tell Someone

There is something powerful about sharing your goals with others. There's a nice supportive accountability network that comes with communicating your hopes and desires to grow. They can be a great source of encouragement and remind you in a loving and healthy way of the goals we tend to lose sight of. Let's be honest, no one wants to run into that friend who asks how you're doing on your goals only to report you haven't started. Telling someone your plans will help you move forward. So, who will you tell? What will you tell yourself to stay on track?

Applying the feedback we receive to our everyday life is not as easy as many believe it to be. Some people believe that it's as simple as doing whatever it is someone else tells them to do. Mindlessly reacting to feedback can be dangerous. My mother would say, "if they told you to jump off of a bridge, would you do it?" She was challenging us as children to listen to others but to think for ourselves. It is important to engage your heart and head in the process. Using both your IQ and EQ will help you make meaningful and long-lasting changes.

Applying feedback also requires that we think deeply and broadly about what we need in order to successfully implement the feedback we've encountered. Assessing your needs, creating a plan, and telling others about it will increase the likelihood of the behavior being incorporated into your everyday life.

CHAPTER NINE

Remote Feedback

"Encouragement is oxygen for the sourl."— John Maxwell

Telecommuting is an option that affords people flexibility in their work location, an option desired by many. In 2016, 43% of Americans worked remotely in some capacity (Gallup, 2017). Today, there has been a seismic shift in the use of remote work with nearly seven in 10 employees who are working remotely all or part of the time. Organizations across the globe are rethinking where work should be done and how to do it effectively.

So how does this impact feedback? Have you thought about what happens to the feedback dynamic when it intersects with remote communication channels? People across the globe will have to become skilled at delivering, receiving, processing, and applying feedback in ways other than face-to-face. I'll talk you through some tips on how to navigate feedback using remote channels.

The Feedback Ecosystem:

As mentioned in Chapter Two, the feedback ecosystem is important. The Feedback Ecosystem is the environment in which people interact and exchange information. When that environment is remote, you must think more intentionally about the feedback experience. I took the elements of the ecosystem and modified them to be seen through the experience of a remote exchange.

1. Psychological Safety: Psychological safety is the belief that you won't be punished when you make a mistake (Delizonna, 2017). It is the ability to bring your full authentic self to an interaction and feel accepted, respected, and valued. In a remote environment, you want to ensure that people feel safe to contribute their ideas and share their opinions. This is how you harvest the richness of innovation. To do this, you want to be sure that you are inclusive. The intentional inclusion of all voices in a discussion can foster psychological safety and trust. If you have some people who are in-person while others are remote, be sure to include them first and not last so that they do not feel like an afterthought. Creating safe spaces for everyone to contribute is key!

2. Trust-Equity: The key is to build up some trust-equity so that when it comes time for feedback conversations, no one has to question each other's motives, defend themselves, or dismiss

the feedback. Both parties can assume positive intent because there is a mutual belief, respect, and trust in one another. To build trust-equity remotely, you can start by trusting that they are performing their job duties even though they are not in your visible line of sight. Micromanagement is a sure way to reduce trust and make giving feedback in the future more challenging.

3. Ontological Humility: Ontological humility is the acknowledgment that the truth does not lie with you alone and that others have equally valid perspectives that should be heard and considered (Kofman, 2006). When you have an ecosystem where there is no hierarchy to consider when it comes to perspectives, this can create a very healthy environment. Doing a round-robin share-out of ideas is a great way to hear the perspectives of others. Asking people to share the pros and cons of the ideas as they relate to the problem that you are trying to solve can be helpful as well. This will help foster a culture where you build off of cognitive diversity.

4. Bidirectional Feedback: It is important to take the lid off of feedback and make it bidirectional. That is, feedback can flow from top to bottom and from bottom to top. Incorporating questions like, "what is one thing I can do to better support you?" or "what do you have on your plate that I can help you with?" can open up the gates of communication and allow the exchange to feel bidirectional.

General guidelines for delivering feedback remotely:

1. Check In: Be focused on the relationship, not the feedback. Be sure to still check in with the individual to see how they are doing. Remember, keep the humanity in the experience. If it's truly about them, make this time count. Every interaction is an opportunity to strengthen your relationship. Connect with them and let them know they matter.

2. Address FOMO: Being remote can feel isolating and lonely. People may have a Fear Of Missing Out. Take the time to fill them in on what you've been up to so that they feel connected to what's happening in your space. This can reinforce safety and build trust-equity.

3. Recognize: Take a moment to acknowledge their accomplishments since your last conversation. Feeling seen is important when you are not co-located. Taking the time to demonstrate that you've seen their work and acknowledge what they've done well is critical.

4. Deliver the G.I.F.T.—Give, Intend, Focus, Timely. Give the feedback directly to them; do not CC anyone if it's via email. Be clear about your intentions—focus it on behavior, effects and solutions, and be sure that it is timely. Revisit Chapter Four for details.

5. Offer support: Being remote can feel very lonely. It can even feel like you are on an island all by yourself. Be sure to offer support as they work to implement the feedback. Be sure to let them know that you're available in between formal meetings if they need anything.

Remote Communication Channels

When delivering feedback, a voice-to-voice communication is always ideal. It's a great opportunity for fostering connections, building relationships, and opening the door to some bidirectional feedback. If you have limited time and want to be more intentional about how you pass along feedback via remote channels, here's a few tips that might guide your thinking as you try to identify the right communication channel for your feedback.

The first thing to consider is what you're trying to impact: Behavioral Feedback or Technical Feedback. Behavioral feedback is focused on how something is done and technical feedback is focused on what is done. For example, giving feedback on someone's presentation skills is behavioral feedback. Feedback on the organization and contents of the presentation is technical feedback.

The second thing to consider is the complexity of the feedback: High Complexity or Low Complexity. High Complexity feedback is something that requires multiple perspectives, inquiry, discussion, collaboration, and coaching. Low Complexity feedback is something that only requires one perspective, independent reflection, and receiver autonomy and empowerment. For example, giving someone feedback on overcoming nerves, commanding and engaging the audience might be considered High Complexity depending on the individual's level of experience. Giving someone feedback on which order the presentation slides should go in would be considered Low Complexity.

Remote Feedback Matrix

	Low Complexity Feedback	High Complexity Feedback
Behavioral Feedback	Email	Video Call Phone Call
Technical Feedback	Email	Video Call Phone Call

Video/Phone Call: Behavioral Feedback, Technical Feedback, High Complexity

These methods should be used when your feedback requires two-way dialogue and you want to collaborate on the solution. The video aspect makes the discussion flow a bit easier as you have the ability to read the social cues and body language to ensure that you reduce instances of speaking over the other person. In addition, the body language helps you to better understand their perspective and gauge how they are receiving the feedback.

Email: Email is a good way to deliver feedback if focused primarily on facts and recommended steps to take. If it requires a great deal of discussion or if you anticipate a need to ask several clarifying questions, phone or video call would be most appropriate. If you feel as though your email has the appearance of a dissertation, you might want to delete the email and schedule a meeting to discuss. When you are a remote employee, receiving a lengthy email of that nature might feel intimidating. It might impact the appearance of psychological safety, depending on the tone of the email, because it can feel like a very long reprimand.

Communication Channels to Avoid for Constructive Feedback:

Unless you are providing positive feedback, avoid:
- Direct Messages
- Instant Messages
- Text Messages
- Social Media

Whether remote or face-to-face, feedback is critical to the human experience. As you continue your journey toward becoming more intentional about feedback, remember feedback is about learning and not about failure. Jennifer Lim said, "Mistakes are proof you are trying." Developing a feedback mentality will give you the mindset needed to give yourself permission to try and activate your learning. Developing a healthy feedback mentality will take work, a lot of work. Are you ready to do the work? Since you've made it to this part of the book, it is proof that you have it in you to relentlessly pursue your highest potential. When you conquer the complexities of feedback and develop a feedback mentality, I have no doubt that you will be on the path to unlocking your potential, discovering your purpose, and help others do the same! It has been said that a journey of a thousand miles begins with a single step. Congratulations, you've taken the first step.

Want more Feedback Mentality?

The Feedback Mentality Group is dedicated to developing the knowledge, skills, and mindsets needed to leverage feedback in personal and professional settings.

Visit **www.feedbackmentality.com** to learn more about how we can support your development.

Training	• E-Learning courses to guide your development at your own pace or synchonous workshops for teams
Speaking	• Dr. Williams will bring a powerful and dynamic keynote on the importance of a feedback culture and a healthy feedback mentality
Coaching	• Preparing to deliver feedback? Having difficulty processing feedback. Schedule 1-1 coaching sessions to assist with rapid skill development
Book Club	• Order a few books and explore the world of feedback with your closest friends. We will provide you with a book club guide to help you get started
Certification	• Get certified in the feedback mentality content and feel empowered to improve the feedback culture within your own communities

Connect with us:

Facebook: @feedbackmentality

Instagram: @feedback_mentality

Twitter: @FeedbackMental1

Email: info@feedbackmentality.com

Website: www.feedbackmentality.com

Acknowledgements

To my loving husband, Kevin. Words cannot express how grateful I am to God for placing you in my life. You truly complete me and push me to be better each day. This book would not be possible without you. Thank you for always believing in me, investing in my dreams, and pushing me to fully step into my purpose. Your prayers, encouragement, support, and feedback helped to move this work from my heart to my hands. I love you, always!

To my wonderful friends and colleagues who contributed their stories to this book: Simone E. Davis, Dr. Cecil Wright, Cameron Thomas, and Margi Mejia. Thank you for answering the call and being willing to share your stories without hesitation. It means a lot to have people who are willing to believe in your dreams and join you on the journey. Your stories truly complete this book. I appreciate each of you!

To the amazing people in my life who took the time to give me early feedback on the book: Denise August, Temeka

Smith, Stephanie Williams, Nichelle Singleton, Heather Marr, and Joslyn Jackson. I appreciate your radical attention to detail and willingness to support. It means more to me than you'll ever know. Your early feedback gave me the motivation I needed to continue. Thank you so much!

To all of the people in my life who gave me feedback over the course of my life, thank you for your courage and candor. Your feedback over the years has shaped me into the woman I am today and the woman I hope to become in the future. I truly believe I am a better person because of you! Thank you!

Glossary

Feedback: Information that gives insight into how someone perceives something or someone. This information can be about the past or present and can be used to influence the future.

Feedback Baggage: Past negative experiences or ideas related to feedback that might weigh a person down and keep them from being open to feedback.

Feedback Blocking: Feedback blocking is when someone is unwilling to have a two-way feedback exchange. It is when feedback is one-directional and not bidirectional.

Feedback Ecosystem: The environment in which people interact and exchange information; the environment in which feedback occurs.

Feedback Fatigue: The act of becoming mentally and emotionally tired from constantly scanning your environment and finding opportunities to improve.

Feedback Hoarder: The act of withholding feedback from others.

Feedback Mentality: A mindset about feedback

Feedback Muscle: The mental and emotional strength required to deliver, receive, process, and apply feedback.

Delivering Feedback: The physical act of giving feedback to others.

Receiving Feedback: The physical act of receiving feedback from others.

Processing Feedback: The mental act of analyzing the internal narrative attached to feedback.

Applying Feedback: The process of prioritizing and acting on feedback.

Sponge Mentality: The unconscious process of holding onto all feedback you encounter regardless of their value.

Strainer Mentality: The conscious process of SIFTing through constructive feedback, identifying learning, and releasing the feedback that no longer serves you.

Sources

Business Balls. 2019. Maslow's Hierarchy of Needs Retrieved from https://www.businessballs.com/self-awareness maslows-hierarchy-of-needs/

Business Balls. 2019. Mehrabian's Communication Theory: Verbal, Non-Verbal, Body Language. Retrieved from https://www.businessballs.com/communication-skills/mehrabians-com-munication-theory-verbal-non-verbal-body-language/

Center for Creative Leadership. 2020. How to give the most effective feedback. Retrieved from https://www.ccl.org/articles/leading-effectively-articles/review-time-how-to-give-feedback/

Delizonna, L. 2017. High-Performing Teams Need Psychological Safety. Here's How To Create It. Retrieved from https://hbr.org/2017/08/high-performing-teams-need-psycho-logical-safety-heres-how-to-create-it

Gallup. 2017. State of the American Workplace. Retrieved from https://www.gallup.com/workplace/238085/state-american-workplace-report-2017.aspx

Gallup. 2018. Why employees are fed up with feedback. Retrieved from https://www.gallup.com/workplace/267251/why-employees-fed-feedback.aspx

Gallup. 2019. Feedback is not enough. Retrieved from https://www.gallup.com/workplace/257582/feedback-not-enough.aspx#:~:text=Gallup%20has%20found%20that%20only,working%20the%20way%20it%20should.&text=When%20most%20organizations%20had%20hierarchical,making%20method%2C%20feedback%20was%20paramount.

Gallup. 2020. Reviewing remote work in the U.S. under COVID. Retrieved from https://news.gallup.com/poll/311375/reviewing-remote-work-covid.aspx

Gallup. 2020. COVID-19 Has My Teams Working Remotely: A Guide for Leaders. Retrieved from https://www.gallup.com/workplace/288956/covid-teams-working-remotely-guide-leaders.aspx

Gallup. 2020. What meaningful feedback means to millennials. Retrieved from https://www.gallup.com/workplace/284081/meaningful-feedback-means-millennials.aspx

Harvard Business Review. 2014. Your employees want the negative feedback you hate to give. Retrieved from https://hbr.org/2014/01/your-employees-want-the-negative-feedback-you-hate-to-give

Harvard Business Review. 2017. Why Do So Many Managers Avoid Giving Praise? Retrieved from https://hbr.org/2017/05/why-do-so-many-managers-avoid-giving-praise#:~:text=One%20of%20the%20most%20difficult,admitted%20that%20they%20avoid%20it.

Hoffman Institute. 2020. Ten Secrets of 100% Healthy People. Retrieved from https://www.hoffmaninstitute.co.uk/10-secrets-of-healthy-people/

Kofman, F. 2006. *Conscious business: how to build value through values.* Boulder, CO: Sounds True.

Lyubomirsky S. and Nolen-Hoeksema S. 1995. "Effects of self-focused rumination on negative thinking and interpersonal problem solving." *J Personal Soc Psychol* 69:176–190. doi: 10.1037/0022-3514.69.1.176.

Merriam-Webster. n.d. Feedback. In *Merriam-Webster.com dictionary*. Retrieved July 10, 2020, from https://www.merriam-webster.com/dictionary/feedback

Merriam-Webster. n.d. Mentality. In *Merriam-Webster.com* dictionary. Retrieved July 10, 2020, from https://www.merriam-webster.com/dictionary/mentality

Merriam-Webster. n.d. Trust. In *Merriam-Webster.com* dictionary. Retrieved July 11, 2020, from https://www.merriam-webster.com/dictionary/trust

Musser, C. 2019. Give employees the right kind of feedback at the right time. Retrieved from https://www.gallup.com/workplace/268937/give-employees-right-kind-feedback-right-time.aspx

Nolen-Hoeksema, S., Wisco, B. E., and Lyubomirsky, S. 2008. Rethinking Rumination. *Perspectives on Psychological Science* 3(5): 400–424. https://doi.org/10.1111/j.1745-6924.2008.00088.x

OfficeVibe. 2020. The state of employee feedback. Retrieved from https://officevibe.com/employee-engagement-solution/employee-feedback#:~:text=Feedback%20statistics&text=23%25%20of%20employees%20are%20unsatisfied,they%20get%20is%20not%20specific.

Ranganathan, V., Siemionow, V., Sahgal, V., and Yue, G. 2016. From mental power to muscle power—gaining strength by using the mind. Retrieved from https://www.sciencedirect.com/science/article/abs/pii/S0028393203003257?via%3Dihub

Whiteman, R. and Mangels, J. 2016. Rumination and rebound from failure as a function of gender and time on task. *Brain Sciences* 6(1): 7. MDPI AG. Retrieved from http://dx.doi.org/10.3390/brainsci6010007